What Your Colleages Are Saying . . .

"A common refrain from many educators when they see new technology is 'That looks great, but does anyone really use it?' In *Classroom in the Cloud,* Jared Covili and Nick Provenzano not only answer this question with a resounding 'Yes,' they supply real-world anecdotes and direct quotes from teachers and students about the amazing Cloud-based applications they share. Want innovative tools and practices? It's in here. Want step-by-step instruction for implementation? You've got it. Want an array of tools for all grade levels and subjects? It's covered. Best of all, this book provides powerful Cloud-based learning tools and outstanding narratives from two of the most renowned EdTech gurus in the business. Covili and Provenzano have written the go-to guide for Cloud-based learning. The classroom may now be in the Cloud, but this book will be at my side any time I need tech tools that are creative, easy-to-use, and fun for teaching and learning."

—**Mark Barnes,** Author, *Teaching the iStudent* and *5 Skills for the Global Learner*

"Covili and Provenzano have provided a detailed, easy-to-read book for both novice and expert teachers. The in-the-trenches examples of quality tools will help many teachers enhance, engage, and energize their classrooms. Teachers who are moving into 1:1 classroom settings will be enlightened by the student voices featured in this book. I will be using this book in my work with teachers and students as they move to the Cloud!"

—**Harry Dickens,** Author, *Apps for Learning, Middle School* and *Apps for Learning: 40 Best iPad/iPod Touch/iPhone Apps for High School Classrooms*

"This book, written by two expert educators, is exactly what every district needs to support the innovative teaching that Cloud computing can create. With its creative projects and tested ideas from classrooms around the world, *Classroom in the Cloud* is a must-read for any district looking to start their Cloud computing journey or have better implementation of tools they already use."

—**Pernille Ripp,** Author and Seventh-Grade Teacher

"It's more important today than ever before for educators to look beyond the walls of their classrooms and connect with other colleagues in their buildings and across the globe. In *Classroom in the Cloud*, educators at any level of experience will be equipped with the tools necessary to make meaningful connections and find the best tools to enhance and improve their teaching practices."

—**Steven Anderson,** Author,
The Relevant Educator and *Content Curation*

"This work is clear, concise, and straight to the point. If you're looking for practical tools that you can actually use in a classroom, this book is for you. It demystifies the Cloud for those new to the digital journey while also providing some great gems for those who are already highly proficient at Cloud-based tools. I love the implied message here that a classroom in the Cloud is essentially a creative classroom where students can share their work with the world."

—**John T. Spencer,** Speaker, Author, and Professor of
Instructional Technology, George Fox University

"Covili and Provenzano have done a fantastic job of putting together this resource of Cloud-based tools for teaching and learning. It is a valuable asset to any new teacher, veteran teacher, administrator, or IT leader. If you want to truly take your schools and classrooms to the Cloud, this book will get you there!"

—**Kyle Pace,** Instructional Technology Specialist

Classroom in the Cloud

Innovative Ideas for Higher Level Learning

Jared Covili

Nicholas Provenzano

Foreword by Adam Bellow

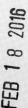

CORWIN

A SAGE Company

FOR INFORMATION:

Corwin

A SAGE Company

2455 Teller Road

Thousand Oaks, California 91320

(800) 233-9936

www.corwin.com

SAGE Publications Ltd.

1 Oliver's Yard

55 City Road

London EC1Y 1SP

United Kingdom

SAGE Publications India Pvt. Ltd.

B 1/I 1 Mohan Cooperative Industrial Area

Mathura Road, New Delhi 110 044

India

SAGE Publications Asia-Pacific Pte. Ltd.

3 Church Street

#10-04 Samsung Hub

Singapore 049483

Executive Editor: Arnis Burvikovs

Signing Editor: Desirée A. Bartlett

Editorial Assistant: Andrew Olson

Production Editor: Melanie Birdsall

Copy Editor: Deanna Noga

Typesetter: C&M Digitals (P) Ltd.

Proofreader: Alison Syring

Indexer: Wendy Allex

Cover Designer: Gail Buschman

Marketing Manager: Stephanie Trkay

Printed in the United States of America

Library of Congress Cataloging-in-Publication Data

Names: Covili, Jared, author. | Provenzano, Nicholas, author.

Title: Classroom in the cloud : innovative ideas for higher level learning/Jared Covili, Nicholas Provenzano; foreword by Adam Bellow.

Description: Thousand Oaks, California: Corwin, [2016] | Includes bibliographical references and index.

Identifiers: LCCN 2015027597 | ISBN 9781483319803 (pbk. : alk. paper)

Subjects: LCSH: Educational technology. | Educational innovations. | Cloud computing.

Classification: LCC LB1028.3 .C73 2016 | DDC 371.33—dc23 LC record available at http://lccn.loc.gov/2015027597

This book is printed on acid-free paper.

15 16 17 18 19 10 9 8 7 6 5 4 3 2 1

Contents

Foreword

We live and teach in a truly amazing time. Every day we have a chance to learn and share in ways that we couldn't have imagined just a few short years ago. These learning opportunities are fueled in large part by a seemingly ever-increasing amount of technology that grows more affordable overtime. It would be hard to imagine a life without our smartphones, streaming media that provides on-demand access to anything we could imagine reading, watching, or listening to, or interacting with, and of course the idea of a connected network of not just machines, but also people to share ideas and learn from one another. It is because of the connected world, specifically Twitter, that I had the good fortune to be introduced to the talented authors of this book. Jared and Nick are two educators who took to social media to share their knowledge and passion for educational technology.

Congratulations on purchasing this book! You have chosen wisely. This book is written by two incredibly passionate educators who are nationally recognized by their ability to weave digital tools into the classroom experience to enhance teaching and learning. As practicing educators, Jared and Nick know what schools are like today. They have also experienced schools before technology was successfully implemented into their classes. They have lived through the implementation process (and any stumbles along the way) and seen what incredible changes are possible when the technology is set in place and students are allowed to harness the power of the tools to unlock their learning potential. Jared and Nick are true educators. They teach, they learn, and they inspire others to do the same. This book is a logical extension of their selfless personas exemplified in blogs, presentations, and their classroom. These gentlemen know of which they write.

In addition to Jared and Nick, you'll learn from other incredible educators today who are also using technology in unique ways that is nothing short of inspiring. The tools curated and discussed in this book are a nice cross-section of some of the options you have available to you in the Cloud. It is easy to search for a "best of" list and be overwhelmed with many options of apps, tools, and so on that can be useful in the classroom, but learning about the tools that have been selected for you here and seeing how they are manipulated to provide structure to real learning objectives will help you form guidelines of how to look at tools and evaluate them as time goes on. It's the "teach a person to fish" mentality that I am referring to here; you are about to learn how to get lots of fish. And thinking critically about tools and how they can work for you and your classrooms or schools is a vital step in implementation. Knowing which ones to try, which ones to abandon, and which ones to stick with is an important skill to learn. Add to the mix the seasoned expertise that these educators have as masters of the art of teaching, and you will quickly see that you are in the right hands.

The book is not a traditional cover-to-cover experience, as our authors explain in just a bit. It can be used as inspiration, reference, and as a guideline for how to think about tools that you haven't even heard of yet. Because the truth is that excellent teachers with access to malleable tools can create amazing learning experiences and that is what makes it all worth it.

Enjoy!

—**Adam Bellow**
Founder of eduTecher/eduClipper
Plainview, New York

Preface

Technology continues to change the world in which our students live. They are now in a state of constant connectivity—to each other, to information, to the world at large. So why do schools seem to exist in a vacuum? Our classrooms still have a disconnect between the content students learn at school and the world in which students live. A solution many teachers are looking into is the Cloud—an online set of websites and resources that provide students and teachers with immediate access to content and colleagues. By using the Cloud teachers are looking to connect students, engage with content, manage data, cut costs, and improve performance. This book will explore various Cloud-based tools from a K–12 educator's perspective, not simply focusing on how to use the tools, but also answering the larger questions of *Why use these tools?* and *How can my students meet learning standards if they utilize the Cloud?*

Whether you are a new teacher or a veteran teacher, you will find great Cloud-based tools that you can integrate into your class right away. *Down in the Trenches* and *A Student's Views*—we worked very hard to find the best case uses to provide strong examples of how the tool will work not only from the teacher's perspective, but also from the point of view of students. We know that there is tremendous value in having teacher examples when sharing a tool, and we provided those and the teacher's contact information if you have more questions on how to use the tool. This book is hopefully a starting point for you and your exploration into Cloud-based technologies for the classroom.

Administrators will find the Cloud to have several unique advantages for their schools. Regardless of whether you come from the largest school district in your state or you're a brand new charter school with a small staff, we believe this book will help you chart a plan for technology integration with your teachers. The tools in this book will help you maximize the infrastructure you currently have. Whether you are on PCs, Macs, tablets, or BYOD, you will find tools you can use in your situation. And the best part of using these tools is you won't break the budget because all the Cloud tools we profile have free options available. The Cloud will help you set the course for your classrooms and provide access to tools your teachers and students will love!

This book is broken down into four major areas: *Storing in the Cloud, Communicating in the Cloud, Collaborating in the Cloud,* and *Creating in the Cloud.* In each section of the book, we explore different Cloud-based tools educators can use to perform a variety of classroom tasks: including learning assessment, content development, and data management.

As we discuss the various tenets of the Cloud and how the tools relate to learning skills, we hope you'll find this book addresses three essential areas for K–12 educators:

1. Which Cloud-based tools are essential for achieving learning objectives?

2. How can these tools improve learning and help teachers in their everyday classroom activities?

3. What are some practical lesson plan activities teachers can use with different Cloud-based tools as part of their student-centered projects?

To help in digesting key points and features in the book, each chapter focuses on a classroom activity or project that is separated with its own unique heading. This makes the step-by-step instructions easier to find and follow. At the end of each chapter, you'll find another highlight for teachers—*Taking It to a Higher Level.* This is a set of quick ideas meant to further your use of the tools and provide an additional framework for classroom application. You will also find a useful resource—*If You Like That, Try This*—at the end of the book. This section of the book is designed to help teachers find similar resources to those shared in the book, in case of district filters, cost, or other hindering factors.

Another important feature found throughout the book is the use of screen captures. These images are designed to help illustrate concepts and provide guidance for accomplishing activities. The screen captures are time sensitive, so their content won't be relevant forever, but they provide a valuable resource to help educators visualize different Cloud-based tools in action.

Classroom in the Cloud is meant to be a useful resource for the 21st century educator; one that provides a variety of ideas to help teachers address various standards and increase student productivity and learning. As we take learning into the Cloud, we hope you'll see how these tools can take your classroom to a higher level.

Acknowledgments

We would like to thank the following groups for their help and support:

To all the teachers, administrators, technology trainers, and all around educators—we really appreciate your willingness to share your stories with us. This book wouldn't be the same without your amazing examples and the great work you do in education!

To the students who shared their opinions—you provided unique insights into the impact that the Cloud has on your learning. Your practical observations helped us show how tools can open the door to learning.

To the companies who provided us access to share their tools—we are so grateful you've created amazing tools that promote learning. It's easy to share the stories of educators who succeed using your incredible tools. Keep building great resources and teachers will continue to sing your praises!

Publisher's Acknowledgments

Corwin would like to thank the following individuals for their editorial insight and guidance:

April Keck DeGennaro, Gifted Education Teacher
Peeples Elementary School
Fayetteville, GA

Steve Dembo, Director of Social Media & Online Community, Discovery Education
Adjunct Professor, Wilkes University
Chicago, IL

Delsia Malone, Principal
W. E. Striplin Elementary School
Gadsden, AL

Dustin Summey, Instructional Design Specialist
Instructional Development Center
University of Central Arkansas
Conway, AR

About the Authors

Jared Covili is a statewide technology trainer for the Utah Education Network. He specializes in teaching strategies for classroom integration of technology such as Google resources, Web 2.0 learning tools, geospatial learning, social media tools, and digital devices. His background is in secondary education where Jared was a Language Arts teacher at the high school level.

Besides his work at UEN, Jared is also an adjunct faculty member of the College of Education at the University of Utah, where he teaches technology integration classes to undergraduate students. Jared served as the President of UCET (Utah Coalition for Educational Technology) in 2011–2012. His first book, *Going Google: Powerful Tools for 21st Century Learning*, was published by Corwin in March 2012. You can find Jared on Twitter at @covili.

Nicholas Provenzano is a high school English teacher and an education blogger. He writes on his website, TheNerdyTeacher.com, Edutopia.org, the ISTE blog, as well as several other prominent educational websites. He has been featured on CNN.com, in *The New York Times*, *Consumer Reports*, and many other media outlets.

In 2013, he was awarded the Technology Teacher of the Year by MACUL and ISTE based on his efforts to integrate technology into the classroom. In the summer of 2014, Nicholas became a Google Certified Teacher. Nicholas can be found tweeting plenty of nerdy ideas on Twitter at @TheNerdyTeacher.

*For my mother Kaaren, who always believed in me—even
when I had my head in the clouds.*

—Jared

*To Jenny, my beautiful wife who supports
me in all my crazy adventures.*

*To Leonardo, the leader in blue and my amazing son
who keeps me grounded and laughing.*

*To my parents, Dr. Robert and Susan, for
always pushing me to be better.*

*To my amazing PLN for supporting me on this venture and
so many. I would not be here without all the things you do for me
over the course of any given day. You complete me.*

*To my amazing students. You will always be "my kids"
long after you graduate. You are the "Dream Team"
any teacher would be lucky to have.*

—Nick

Introduction

What Is the Cloud Classroom?

The web has changed the way in which teachers and students access information and complete assignments. For years teachers and students could only work on a project from a specific computer, one that had the right software, the right memory, and the right hardware. With the advent of the Cloud, we have seen how schools have leveraged online storage and tools that are accessible on any device, regardless of the software or platform. This gives teachers and students access to their work from anywhere. They can work on projects at any time. They can complete assignments on any device. Teachers and students who leverage the Cloud are better able to learn from their peers. They can access educational materials from a variety of resources. They save time and energy, maximizing the web and the different Cloud-based tools they find there.

What Is the Cloud?

Many people reference the idea of Cloud computing, while treating it like a mystical force. When asked they simply say, "My stuff is saved up there," without really knowing where *there* is. The Cloud may mean different things to different people. Cloud computing can be as simple as a shared network drive at school that serves only the staff and students, or it can as complex as a system that encompasses millions of users from around the world.

Cloud computing has been defined by the National Institute of Standards & Technology as

> a model for enabling ubiquitous, convenient, on-demand network access to a shared pool of configurable computing resources (e.g., networks, servers, storage, applications, and

services) that can be rapidly provisioned and released with
minimal management effort or service provider interaction.
(Edutopia, n.d.)

In its simplest form Cloud computing has a few key components:

- Information is stored on remote servers, not on local hard
  drives.
- Information can be accessed with a secure login and password.
- Information can be public or private, depending on the user's
  preference.
- Information can be accessed on a variety of platforms and
  devices.

How Is the Cloud Changing Schools?

In an increasingly "on-demand" society, the role of Cloud computing
becomes even more important in today's classroom. Learning was
once seen as something that took place from 8 a.m. to 3 p.m. at the
local schoolhouse; now it is a 24-hour a day continuous opportunity
for connecting and discussing new ideas and content.

Secretary of Education Arne Duncan discussed the changing role
of the classroom in lives of our students.

What will school be like in five years from now? In ten
years from now? Will it still be thought of in terms of traditional brick and mortar? Kids may be learning as much
from their cell phones at 9 o'clock at night as they are in the
classroom. (*Frontline*, 2010)

Schools of tomorrow will rely less on the questions of "where are
students learning—what are they learning on" and more on the question of "what are students learning." Online learning continues to
grow and its impact is changing the face of education. In fact, the
digital divide may have less to do with what kind of hardware a
school or district has and more to do with what access to the Internet
a student has. The Cloud has made the computing device rather inter-
changeable and unimportant—connectivity is what matters most.

The Cloud-based classroom will have a huge impact of the types
of technology tools we see in students' hands. Rather than having
schools and districts purchase high-end networking hardware, students can access content on smaller, mobile devices they bring from

home. Schools will invest less money maintaining dedicated computer labs and more resources will be used to purchase portable labs, full of entry-level tablets and laptops, such as the Google Chromebook. With more resources going toward online content and curriculum rather than hardware, educators can have a greater impact on student learning.

Why Use the Cloud?

> The nature of the cloud also allows students to share beyond ideas. They can share education infrastructure and tools. Schools can spend less on new software, text books and latest-expensive learning material. This will not only help schools leverage tight budgets, but will also enable students to access vital information. (CloudTweaks, 2012)

Let's look at some of the benefits of the Cloud in today's schools.

Cost Effective

Many Cloud-based solutions are no cost to low cost. Solutions like Google Apps for Education or Microsoft Live 365 can provide schools with powerful data services for FREE. For school districts, this can alleviate the heavy cost of servers and maintenance. Large districts can save thousands of dollars by moving the data from their servers. Small districts can get access to large-scale solutions without dedicating overworked personnel and resources. For each, IT staff and equipment can be repurposed for tasks other than e-mail and server maintenance. These savings will directly impact classrooms because teachers will have additional resources for instruction, not infrastructure.

Having companies providing districts and schools Cloud-based services offers other cost savings that aren't always recognized in the initial rollout. By leveraging the scale of Cloud-based services, a district gains access to levels of security and support that were previously out of reach. For districts that are part of the Cloud's network, it's one of the many cost saving measures that comes standard.

In addition to saving money on technology infrastructure, Cloud solutions can save district budgets through access to online word processing tools. Money doesn't have to be spent on desktop software when comparable programs can be accessed online. Additionally, districts don't need to roll out the latest versions of software to every machine, because the new version is already in the Cloud. This may seem like a simple savings early on, but when you consider the Cloud automatically updates to the latest version of a program, the cost savings grows over time.

Access

One of the greatest benefits of the Cloud for our schools is the ability to access content anytime, from anywhere, on any device. The end of the school day shouldn't create a wall for students, those trying to access and work on their assignments during off-school hours. With projects living in the Cloud, students can easily continue their work once they return home. The Cloud backs up all their assignments, so the students see little difference between what they started at school and what they develop at home.

We often hear of the digital divide (those who have access to technology and those who do not) being a key factor in determining student and school success. Cloud-based tools level the playing field by providing the same access to content and applications. Students have the most recent versions of the online programs so they can work seamlessly with one another.

A recent US Department of Education Initiative called Connect ED is taking advantage of the Internet as a tool to improve connectivity and expand access for students.

> Rural communities will experience some of the greatest benefits of new education technologies, as ConnectED will help provide learning opportunities to level the playing field for rural students. Both small districts and large can benefit from distance learning and students can take classes from instructors from anywhere in the world. (The White House, n.d., p. 2)

Access also deals with the issue of scalability. As districts grow or shrink, Cloud solutions are easy to adapt to the changing population. Since many Cloud tools are free, districts can customize the scale of operations to ensure they get the level of access they need.

Increased Collaboration

Without requiring students to have the same software, collaboration increases within the Cloud. Imagine students working on the same project, from home, at the same time. They have the ability to share ideas with one another and bring those thoughts to fruition by working in the project collectively.

Collaborating in the Cloud can bring the world to your classroom because you can have your students working with kids from across the globe. Since location is no longer a barrier, imagine having students in Kansas working on a climate science project with their counterparts in Brazil. The Cloud can have these students not only working in the same documents, but also seeing and talking with one another as though they are in the same room (and in a sense, they are).

> Collaborative projects really make for an excellent education experience not only because students bounce ideas off each other and improve each other's writing skills, but also because the process itself teaches them how to work well with others—a valuable skill for everyone. (Richard Ellwood, Technology Coordinator and Digital Arts Teacher, Columbia Secondary School)

Individualized Instruction

> Digital differentiation is all about designing and facilitating student driven learning experiences that are fueled by standard based essential questions and powered by digital tools to provide students with flexible learning paths for success. (Educational Technology and Mobile Learning, n.d.)

With student data being stored in the Cloud, it provides teachers and schools with instant information. Having access to large amounts of data provides instructors a snapshot into a student's preferred method of learning. Can you imagine if each student had their own individual education plan (IEP)?

Jim Peterson, a teacher in Bloomington, IL, discussed how using Cloud tools have helped him work with students in more individualized ways:

> The upshot of storing data in one location is that it can be used to tailor specific curricula to each child. If Johnny's data suggests that he's a tactile learner and he's failing math, inBloom might suggest a particular teaching approach. This is all about building personalized learning environments. (Fink & Segal, 2013)

Using the Cloud to access student data, one quickly sees how districts can leverage online information systems to help them make "data-driven decisions."

Standardized Assessments

Since schools and districts can share resources online, implementing large- and small-scale assessments has never been easier. This allows testing to be uniform across the different locations and helps ensure a level of fairness through standardizing the materials.

As more and more urban school districts continue to search for answers to stagnant test scores and high drop-out rates, Cloud computing-powered classrooms have become the Holy Grail of most principals' wish lists (Hausman, 2013). Let's take the example of the Mooresville School District in Mooresville, North Carolina.

The Mooresville Graded School District distributes one device per student (Grades 3–12) and uses predominantly digital curriculum content. All teachers are trained on how to integrate technology into their teaching. Since beginning the shift to greater use of technology, learning in Mooresville has changed. As superintendent Mark Edwards has said, "This is not about the technology. It's not about the box. It's about changing the culture of instruction—preparing students for their future, not our past."

In the classroom, students now collaborate in small groups rather than listening to lectures. They are using individualized software that functions like a personal tutor, adapting to their pace of learning. Teachers receive immediate feedback on students' progress and can better direct their lessons and their teaching to meet each student's needs.

> There has been strong evidence of success in Mooresville. The district's graduation rate was 91 percent in 2011, up from 80 percent in 2008. On state tests in reading, math and science, an average of 88 percent of students across grades and subjects met proficiency standards, compared with 73 percent three years ago. Mooresville ranks 100th out of 115 districts in North Carolina regarding dollars spent per student, but it is now third in test scores and second in graduation rates. (The White House, n.d.)

Flipping the Classroom

Over the past couple of years there has been a movement of using the Cloud to provide content instruction to students. Rather than having teachers spend the entire school day in basic instruction, those tasks should be off-loaded to the Cloud, a place where students can engage with content and colleagues. The classroom can then become the laboratory—the application of content knowledge.

With overcrowded classrooms, having students learn content in the Cloud provides educators with the ability to customize classroom activities to meet individual student needs. Bill Gates recently argued that flipping the classroom to Cloud-based instruction can help accomplish this. "Today, classes are too big. Lessons are taught the same way to dozens or hundreds of students—each of whom has different learning style. Technology can, and should, change that" (Fink & Segal, 2013).

There are so many different influences the Cloud can have on an educator's classroom. Each of the ideas listed above ties in with one another in a symbiotic relationship. Cost savings can provide room for additional resources. Additional resources can improve a teacher's ability to reach students on an individual level. When each student has individual attention, achievement goes up. This can have a lasting impact on the smaller communities and, ultimately, on our nation as a whole.

Storms in the Cloud

Of course the Cloud isn't always going to work perfectly all the time. There are a few inherent challenges to having students access programs and data online. Issues can range from lost data to compromised information. Here are some key concerns that have been raised by student advocates and various education groups and the ways in which professionals are trying to protect the Cloud.

Internet Reliability

If your school or district switches everything to the Cloud, your ability to learn is only as good as your Internet connection. If your school has trouble maintaining good connectivity, students and teachers can suffer from long periods of downtime.

Many IT experts say that connectivity shouldn't be a hindrance to schools adopting Cloud-based solutions. Take Google spokesperson Tim Drinan, who recently stated, "Google also never takes down its servers or schedules downtime. We guarantee data availability 99.9 percent of the time" (Asher-Schapiro, 2013).

Even with a 99.9 percent guarantee, there are still those times when data is slow to retrieve or access is impossible. It doesn't matter that the Cloud works seemingly all the time if there's one time you need something and you're unable to pull your information from the Internet. This is an issue that is constantly being addressed and one that grows smaller every year. Gone are the days of dial-up access; now it's more about what is online versus how to get online.

Hackers and Security

With data being accessible online there is the risk of outside attacks by groups or individuals. We read of companies being hacked and data being harvested for nefarious purposes. Is this risk too great to take when it comes to our school data? How can the Cloud be safe?

A tool, like Google Apps for Education, is more secure than IT services run by individual K–12 districts, because of the sheer scale of Google's operation. "We have hundreds of engineers responsible for maintaining Google's security apparatus," Tim Drinan explains. "Those engineers are constantly checking for bugs, intrusions, and data leaks" (Asher-Schapiro, 2013).

There is always a risk putting sensitive data online, and schools need to be vigilant in protecting student information. When it comes to large-scale Cloud solutions, the security measures that need to be employed are beyond the scope a regular district can take on its own. At what point do the educational benefits outweigh the security risks?

Privacy and Sharing Information

Another major concern of parents and students is that of data sharing with third parties. When schools begin uploading student data to the Cloud, it raises the question of access—who can see sensitive student data and what can they do with it?

At a recent school board meeting this feeling was voiced. "You're not going to give out my child's information to a third-party corporation to do whatever it is they want to do," Jelani Makarishi argued over whistles and applause from the audience. "The people are not going to have it and we are going to fight back" (Brownstone, 2013).

Data sharing is an essential feature of Cloud computing. It provides schools with the ability to draw in additional resources and people to help work with individual students. Imagine the following scenario:

> If a student changes schools, that student's data would follow her in a consistent format. Then, it's theoretically easier to understand a student's—or even an entire student group's—performance over time throughout their educational career, because all of that granular data is in one bucket. (Catalano, 2013)

Schools and teachers need to be able to share data with one another. It provides a level of understanding to the needs of each student that was impossible only a decade ago. While data should be shared, it is important to note that it should not be sold to third parties. Student data should improve student learning, not be part of a commercial endeavor.

Clouds, Not Factories

The modern classroom structure was initially based on the industrial age factory model. Our nation needed its children to become contributing members of the working class. Today's children *are* capable of this, but they are capable of *much more.*

In 2013, Sugata Mitra was awarded the TED prize for his work on creating Cloud-based classrooms. In his acceptance speech he stated,

> Kids will help us explore a range of Cloud-based, scalable approaches to self-directed learning. A global network of educators and retired teachers will support and engage the children through the web. In the networked age, we need schools, not structured like factories, but like clouds.

How to Use This Book

Classroom in the Cloud isn't like your typical *"how to"* textbook. Learning how to use the different tools in the Cloud is part of the goal, but you should also come to understand how to use the tools as part of an effective teaching strategy. That being said, this book wasn't designed to be followed from cover to cover, either. Rather, you should be able to scan quickly to any given section of the book to learn more about a specific Cloud tool and its classroom application.

Key book features include the following:

- *Down in the Trenches,* where educators share case studies using Cloud tools in their classroom and school and provide readers with practical examples of lessons that work
- Student insight into application of tools for schoolwork
- Illustrated ideas for implementing a Cloud-based tool in instruction
- Shared tips for *Taking It to a Higher Level* at the end of each chapter
- Suggested resources for further exploration in the section at the end of the book, *If You Like That, Try This*

Innovative Ideas for Higher Level Learning

The premise of this book is simple: Educators want to use the best tools to engage their students and prepare them for their future. Utilizing the Cloud can dramatically alter the scope of learning in the classroom. This book has three core aims for educators:

1. Explore the skills that students will need moving forward in the 21st century.

2. Learn about the different Cloud-based tools from practicing teachers and discover how you can leverage the various resources in your classroom.

3. Identify several classroom projects you can incorporate into your curriculum.

As we learn about the Cloud and the many tools and resources therein, we hope you'll find some new ways to break down the walls of the traditional classroom. In the end, perhaps the greatest thing that can be said of your students is that they have their heads in the Cloud.

1

Storing in the Cloud

The idea of storing your data on a remote server is not new. For years teachers have been able to store their files on local networks and servers. The concept of storing your files on the Internet is one that many saw as a game changer in the past decade. Teachers and students could have access to files beyond the walls of the school, giving them more time to work and better access to learn.

By moving files from these local servers to the web, schools could cut costs of purchasing and maintaining network servers. Now, storing files in the Cloud requires that schools and districts change some traditional ways of thinking when it comes to protecting student data. Using the Cloud will ask us to "trust" the companies we use to house our files and back up our data.

Security

A huge concern for any school or district looking to store student files in the Cloud is security. We need to know that our students' work is safe online and that other parties aren't going to be able to access student information. In this world where data hacking seems to be an everyday occurrence, is it possible for students to feel safe putting their files in the Cloud?

Storing files remotely has been around for quite a while. For years many districts and schools have allowed teachers and students access to shared network drives. This allowed teachers and students to save their work on any computer within the building.

This was a great solution for many teachers because it provided them the ability to store files without having to worry about filling up their computer's hard drive. For students it provided a place to save files to work on later. The files were backed up and stored on shared network servers that were protected and maintained by district or school tech personnel.

Herein lies the problem; districts and schools have limited resources and personnel given the responsibility of protecting student and teacher information from attacks by hackers. Even if your data is behind a local firewall, it is still susceptible to attack from outside parties.

Districts and schools who have moved file storage away from local servers now have greater security than ever before. Rather than a handful of local employees fighting the battle against outside intruders, you have access to thousands of dedicated security experts at companies like Google or Microsoft.

"We back up the data every night, and employ staff that perform regular penetration and audit testing to continuously test the limits of the security apparatus," describes Jim Peterson, technology director at Bloomington (IL) School District 87. "We provide multi-million-dollar levels of security that schools can't afford on their own" (Asher-Schapiro, 2013).

Teachers recognize that the benefits of storing files online outweigh the minimal risks by having those files in the Cloud. Many are willing to take the chance because they see the power of have files available 24/7 through the Internet.

> I think many teachers are saving things in the Cloud without realizing it. Email is in the Cloud, we store pictures there, documents, and major software companies are all following suit behind Google and creating Cloud-based versions of their software. Fortune 500 companies are doing business in the Cloud. Even though nothing is foolproof, the Cloud has become a very viable, secure place. (Kyle Pace, personal communication, September 20, 2014)

Access

Perhaps the largest benefit of storing files in the Cloud is that of access. Our world relies on having instant access to information, and schools are no different. By moving files from a local computer or device and storing them online, teachers and students can have access to their files whenever they need them.

Think back to the way things were a few years ago. Students would be working on a project in the school computer lab. It was nearing the time for the final bell to ring, and students would rush to back up their files for later access. Some would search their bags for a thumb drive so they could save the file, others would hurriedly save their project to the desktop with the hopes of attaching it to an e-mail they would send to themselves. Many students would successfully navigate through this world, some would not.

Now, think of the students' world when their project is stored in the Cloud. The bell is about to ring and the student confidently clicks save (many programs do this automatically). That's it! There's no panic, no frantic search for a device, no workarounds to get past the district firewall. Just a simple save and the project is stored online.

> Before Cloud-based tools my students had to save projects on their network drive. If they wanted to continue working on something at home they would have to email it to themselves because our students were not allowed to use flash drives on school computers. Cloud-based tools not only solved this issue, but it allowed students to create and collaborate easily with other students. (Beth Still, personal communication, September 20, 2014)

The world of technology is in constant evolution. In just the past few years we've seen a dramatic shift from schools with computer labs throughout, to halls being full of students with mobile devices. With the rapid change in technology, we need access to our information using a variety of devices. Students can start a project using a laptop at school and complete it using a tablet at home. The Cloud gives teachers and students access to files, regardless of the device—all you need is an Internet connection.

Capacity

As the information age continues to expand and grow, our need for increased storage is growing as well. Where attaching files to e-mail was sufficient in the past, now our storage needs have increased dramatically. Students regularly work with multimedia files with sizes in hundreds of megabytes (MB). We need access to large storage drives to meet the demand of the modern classroom.

Students using Cloud services now regularly get storage in gigabytes (GB). Enough storage to back up every school project they've ever created. Having increased storage in the Cloud gives them options. They are not limited to a few files here and a few there. For teachers having storage of 30, 50, or even 100 GB means they can back up and save their entire digital library from their school computer.

> Dropbox is my default drive for saving anything and everything. I am able to save space on my local computers and I have constant access to my files. (Jeff McCauley, personal communication, January 17, 2014)

Tools like Dropbox, Google Drive, and Evernote provide schools with some incredible options for storing files online. More than simply backing up student and teacher data, these programs are revolutionizing the ways in which we work online. In the next few chapters, we explore how students and teachers are using Google Drive, Dropbox, and Evernote as effective Cloud-based learning tools.

DROPBOX

Bird's Eye View: Five Things to Know About Dropbox

1. Dropbox provides teachers and students with 2 GB of syncable storage when they use the basic version.

2. Files can be synced to a variety of devices including tablets, laptops, phones, and more.

3. The public folder allows users to share a link to files they want others to access.

4. Dropbox automatically creates a URL for photos.

5. Users can share files with others to create a community folder for easy access.

What Is Dropbox?

Have you ever been working on a file at school and it's time to go home? I'm sure we've all wanted an easy way to take that file home with us without having to e-mail it or save the document to a portable drive. Dropbox is the solution for Cloud storage and sync for all your important files.

Source: ©Dropbox 2014

Dropbox relies on the Cloud to transfer your files from one device to another. Each personal device is connected through a single account you set up. On the computer, you visit Dropbox.com to access your files. On a tablet or mobile device, you can access content through the Dropbox app. Either way, a file is automatically backed up and synced through the Cloud. If I stop mid-sentence on one computer and save the file, it will be saved as-is to any other device connected to the same account.

Dropbox Features

Dropbox has three unique features to upload and share different files with others.

Photos. The photos folder was added to Dropbox a few years ago. At the time it seemed like any other folder in Dropbox, but, on closer inspection, there is a special little feature that makes this folder something special. Any image added to the Photos folder immediately receives a unique URL. This makes sharing your photos a snap.

Camera Uploads. Dropbox wants to be the home for your online photos. Recently an upload feature was added that automatically loads the photos from your devices (cameras, tablets, cell phones, etc.) into a Dropbox folder. This feature can easily be managed if you're already using a photo service, but this is a quick way to get your images online and sharable.

Public. Files uploaded to the Public folder are also easy to share with others, and they are given a URL. This gives teachers a convenient spot to share handouts and more with students.

Storage and Usage

Dropbox provides basic users with 2 GB of storage space. This can be expanded in a couple different ways. One is for users to refer others to the service. For each referral account teachers and students receive 250 MB of additional storage. Dropbox has also provided additional storage for anyone with a .edu e-mail address.

The only file size limitation for files is found using the browser. Using the Upload button at Dropbox.com limits users to files 10 GB or less in size. Other than that, files can be as large as the users remaining storage space. This means you can store and save your large files—no more e-mail being returned because of an attachment that is too big.

Dropbox in the Cloud

Perhaps the biggest benefit to using Dropbox is the ability to sync files to a variety of devices. This is particularly useful with regard to many mobile devices including tablets and phones. Files synced to your Dropbox account are shared across all the devices you use. With many popular mobile devices this may be the only way you can store external files.

Down in the Trenches

Lance Mosier, an eighth-grade history teacher from Nebraska, has been using Dropbox for several years. It has been useful for him to share information with his students and their parents. Let's hear his story:

I have used Dropbox primarily in these ways:

1. **Parents and Students.** Important documents that parents need to know for my class I have placed in a shared Dropbox folder for parents and students to easily access. My syllabus, information about accessing our online textbook, subscribing to my Class Google Calendar, receiving text reminders from Remind101, and accessing my class Twitter Page are all located in my shared Dropbox folder.

2. **Social Studies Department Staff Development.** Another way that I have used Dropbox is in my capacity as Department Chair of Social Studies. Our goal this school year was an increase of use of Primary Sources in our lessons and activities as part of our schoolwide Literacy Professional Development. I created a Dropbox of handouts and resources of "Best Practices" on using Primary Source documents and my staff was encouraged to add lessons, documents, etc. that we could use as a department to further our professional development on using Primary Sources in our classrooms. It became a shared space for teachers to access and use in our PLC discussions throughout the year.

3. **Enrichment/Computer Programming.** The final way that I used Dropbox was with a group of about 19 students who shared in interest in computer programming using the program Scratch (http://scratch.mit.edu). I gave students a mini-lesson on using the Scratch Program to get them started, and made available tutorials and handouts for students to access so they could further their exploration in the world of Scratch. There was no curriculum lesson or connection, but a chance for students to be exposed to some basic programming and self-exploration on the topic.

(Continued)

(Continued)

Lance Mosier

Eighth-Grade
U.S. History Teacher

Omaha, NE

Twitter: @mosier_histgeek
https://twitter.com/little_abe_213

Blog: http://raidersofhistory
.blogspot.com

The nice thing for me about Dropbox is it makes accessing documents and handouts for those who need it easier. Our school district uses Blackboard for our Course Management Platform. What I have discovered for parents was that it takes them too many web clicks to get to the important stuff they need to get to. With Dropbox, I can share my link with parents via e-mail or making a link available on my online website making it easier for parents and students to get key information needed.

For sharing with staff, I have found that Dropbox is much easier than trying to send large massive e-mail through our school's e-mail client. The shared space in the Cloud makes it easier for my staff to access the things they need, or upload files that they would like to share with the rest of our department.

A Student's View

From John B., Grade 11:

Dropbox is a fantastic way to keep all of your important information with you anytime, anywhere. It allows for people to improve their organization skills by keeping everything in one easy-to-use program.

From Hadley R., Grade 9:

I love the fact that you can put almost everything on Dropbox and it automatically shows up on all of your devices. That provides easy access from any place you are.

Why Use Dropbox?

Dropbox is a fantastic solution for teachers and students looking to store files in the Cloud. You have the ability to upload large files online and access them from any Internet-ready device. Dropbox gives you the ability to share your files easily and provide multiple users editing rights to a file. Since Dropbox allows you to retain the original file properties, it maintains the formatting you've done to your documents. Finally, Dropbox makes it simple to send your photos to the Cloud and sharing your images is a breeze. Dropbox is a magic folder that makes organizing your online classroom quick and easy!

Taking It to a Higher Level

• Expand the power of Dropbox using DropItToMe. This website provides teachers with a secure folder for students to use in submitting assignments. The teacher simply creates an account at dropitto. me and then shares his or her account URL with the students. This is will include the teacher's username as part of the URL (i.e., www. dropitto.me/jteacher). At this point, the student will be prompted for the password—you will need to provide the students with the password. After that the student uploads his or her assignment and receives a simple confirmation that the file has been received. That's all there is. You'll find the student documents inside your Dropbox account in a folder labeled DropItToMe.

• Use Dropbox to share files rather than e-mail. Since Dropbox has a file size limit of 10 GB, it is a convenient way to share large files with colleagues or with your students. Most e-mail accounts can't really handle media file attachments so Dropbox is a perfect tool to share videos, student projects, photos, and more.

• Dropbox works with many popular apps for mobile devices. You can easily open files stored in the Dropbox app with a variety of other apps on your iPhone, Droid, and more. Many of the share features for these devices include an export to Dropbox feature to save your mobile projects. Recently, Dropbox added Microsoft Office editing to its capabilities. Now, you can edit Office files while you're still in Dropbox on your tablet!

GOOGLE DRIVE

Bird's Eye View: Five Things to Know About Google Drive

1. Google Drive provides basic users with 15 GB of free storage. Teachers have *unlimited* storage with your Google Apps for Education account.

2. Google Drive allows users to back up all kinds of files to the Cloud: documents, spreadsheets, presentations, PDFs, images, and more.

3. Students and teachers can easily share files to work collaboratively with others.

4. Google Drive can be expanded to include a variety of third-party classroom tools.

5. Google Drive and Google Classroom can work in connection to help students submit assignments.

What Is Google Drive?

A common problem in the digital classroom is file management. Where do I store my files? How do I access my files? What types of files are allowed and available for the software on my machine? Take into account the parameters of having students trying to save and open files at the end of a class period and this problem gets magnified exponentially.

Source: ©Google 2014

Google Drive morphed out of Google Docs in 2012 as a Google Cloud-based storage system for all your files. In addition to storing your online files, Google Drive is also the home for Google's productivity tools: Google Docs, Google Sheets, Google Slides, Google Forms, and Google Drawing. With these tools you and your students can create a variety of original files that can be stored and shared through the Cloud.

Google Drive Features

One of the best features of Google Drive is the ability to share and collaborate on your files in real time. With a click of the share button, any of the files in your Google Drive can be shared with colleagues, students, and more. Better yet, with any of Google's original tools (Google Docs, Sheets, etc.) you can actually collaborate with others in real time. This means your students can all contribute to one document. This is a great way to have students work in groups on the same file. Consider the current alternative: A group of kids all sit around one computer while one student does all the work. No one wins in that scenario! With Google Drive, students can share their files with one another and everyone can contribute at the same time.

Collaborating has also changed between teachers and students. Using Google Drive, teachers can easily share documents with their students. These files can be shared as read only for handouts or editable for group collaborations. With folders, students can quickly share their work with teachers.

Expanding Google Drive

Another great option for using Google Drive in the Cloud is to extend the tools with a variety of third-party applications. These tools can be found and added through the New menu > More > Connect more apps. Once you open the menu you've just unlocked a treasure trove of resources and tools from the Cloud.

The great thing about these apps is that many of the tools are free. Another advantage is that you can use your Google Drive logon to provide you with access and storage for the tools. Some apps that are essential for the Cloud classroom include:

- **Pixlr Editor.** This is a fantastic tool for editing your photos. It is a tool that has many similar features to the popular photo editing tools that users have been using for years.

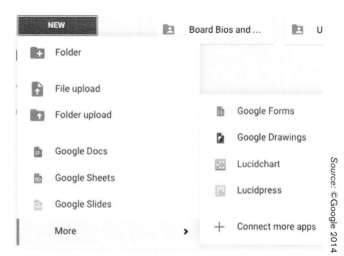

Source: ©Google 2014

- **WeVideo.** Allows users to upload and edit their video in the Cloud. This tool creates finished projects that can be stored in Google Drive, shared online, or saved to devices.

- **MoveNote.** This is a tool for making video-narrated presentations. Cool thing about MoveNote, it allows you to use your Google Slides presentations and add on a video narration alongside the other content.

- **Lucid Chart/Lucid Press.** Two great tools from Lucid. Chart is a tool for creating graphic organizers for your classroom. Press is for desktop publishing and allows your students to create newsletters, brochures, and more.

Mix in Google Classroom

For Google Apps for Education districts, explore adding Google Classroom to maximize your Google Drive. Google Classroom is a one-stop spot for teachers to make announcements and create assignments. Here's the best part: Assignments in Google Classroom can tie directly with your students' Google Drive account. Let's take a closer look at how this works.

When a teacher develops a written assignment in Google Classroom, it automatically creates a Google Doc for his or her students. Students click on the assignment and Google Docs immediately opens, providing them with the ability to create their projects. As the students complete their assignments, a simple click on the Submit button and the teacher now receives the project for review and grading.

The key to this process is that Google Classroom automatically manages document permissions. When the document is assigned to students, the kids have full editing rights to work on the assignment. Once the assignment is submitted to the instructor, the permission instantly changes from editing to viewing rights. Now the permissions change for the instructor, with he or she having rights to make edits, comments, and more.

The process is seamless and happens without any extra effort on the part of the students or the teacher. Once the assignments are created in Google Classroom, the program handles everything else. It's a great tool for everyone!

Down in the Trenches

Google Drive is a favorite tool for teachers and students. One educator using Google Drive as part of her classroom is Rona McIntyre, an instructor from the York University English Language Institute. Read as she shares her story, including a couple examples of classroom activities.

I teach in a university EAP program, but I teach the lowest level. The students are often absolute beginners, and we start at the beginning, with learning the alphabet, names of everyday objects, simple grammar . . . pronouns, nouns, be-verb, simple present and simple past tense. It's an interesting catch-22 because although the students' English level is extremely low, they do want to study academic subjects, and do REAL preparation for university. They want content beyond "dating," "eating out," "family relationships," but at an absolute beginner level. There isn't much prepackaged material on suitable topics, at this level, so I often make my own activities. Many of the students also have little to no computer experience (beyond their cell phones), and if I want to use Google Docs, or others, I need to spend considerable time teaching them basic computer literacy, too. I have had to teach people how to use a mouse, how to type in an address, how to label a file, and so on. Some have told me that they have never touched a computer. The Google Doc activities that I have saved may look very simple to an outside observer, but may represent a monumental accomplishment by the students.

The first activity I'd like to share is a very simple chart titled "Scavenger Hunt" (view it online at http://goo.gl/2TY2sY).

We had been working on plural nouns, the spelling of numbers, and the verbs *have*, *want*, and *need*. I devised this cooperative speaking activity, which incorporates all of those elements.

1. Open with a discussion on what we have and don't have here at YUELI (e.g., students always complain that there is no microwave).

2. Show students my chart on Google Drive and give them the link to access it. I usually prepare a QR code and written link on little slips of paper so they can connect quickly with their cell phones. They do have to sign in to their Google accounts, which we set up earlier in the course. Make sure at least one person from each group can access the chart via phone, tablet, or other device.

(Continued)

(Continued)

3. Send pairs of students out into the hallways of YUELI (it's a bounded environment . . . they can't go too far) to count the items they can find and enter their results in the chart. They can all be in different places simultaneously, and they can see when each group has entered a number. They may leave it or change it if they disagree. I stay in the classroom and watch the results roll in. Because we are always working on spelling, they must enter the data in words, with correct plural forms.

4. Students return to the classroom after 15 minutes, and we have a look at the chart to see if everyone agrees with the numbers and spellings.

5. Ask students to think about the numbers. Together, they must decide whether there are too many, not enough, or something is missing. I ask small groups to make a list of items that are not on the list that they want (list A) or need (list B) here at school.

6. One more whole class consultation to prepare the final "official" wish list, which is given to the class rep to take to the next student rep meeting (organized by management once a month).

The Google Doc is just one small part of this activity, but students like how they can see each other's numbers coming in. The whole activity itself also allows them to feel they have a voice in the student rep meetings and that they can make a difference in the school.

This activity could be adapted for any Scavenger Hunt type of activity.

Another tool I use regularly is Google Forms. Students are required to do weekly reading logs and listening logs outside of class. In the past, I used to hand out paper forms every week (2 forms × 16 students × 8 weeks) and collect them for marking. Students never looked at them again. What a waste of paper! I created the forms in Google Drive and put the links in our Moodle classroom. Now the students just go into Moodle, fill out the form online, and submit it. I get a complete report of all the submissions, and I can give comments in Moodle. Grades go into the grade book, and comments go straight to the students.

Using Google Drive has saved me making photocopies every week, and once I got into the swing of it, I think it has saved me time in marking these two items. These two items do not receive detailed feedback; only a couple of quick comments and advice for the next week. It's really easy. And I can see at a glance what each student has done as the weeks progress.

Check out Rona's projects:

Reading Logs:
http://goo.gl/ihpzEk

Listening Logs:
http://goo.gl/HhfozY

Source: Used with permission of Rona McIntyre.

Rona McIntyre

Instructor

York University English Language Institute

Toronto, Canada

Twitter: @RonaTeacher

Google Drive also is a favorite of Tiffany Whitehead, a Library Media specialist from Baton Rouge, LA. Her school uses Google Drive to help teachers and students work collaboratively with one another. Here's more from the Mighty Little Librarian:

Google Drive helps me connect with my students and teachers, work collaboratively with other educators, and collect and organize data. I love that with Drive I'm always connected to all my documents and projects, no matter what device I am using. The way that all Google's tools are so deeply integrated to work together seamlessly is a thing of beauty.

The Drive tool that I absolutely couldn't live without is Forms. As the librarian, I am constantly collecting information from students and teachers, and Forms makes it possible for me to quickly and efficiently collect and organize data. I recently used Forms to conduct a library survey, soliciting feedback from my 950+ students about our school library program. (See blog post here: http://www.mighty littlelibrarian.com/?p=1072. Feel free to pull anything from the post,

(Continued)

(Continued)

Source: Used with permission of Tiffany Whitehead.

Tiffany Whitehead

School Librarian

Central Middle School

Baton Rouge, LA

Twitter: @librarian_tiff

Website: mightylittlelibrarian.com

Recommended Tool to Explore: Schoology

including pictures.) Forms allowed me to quickly put together a user-friendly form to collect student feedback in a variety of formats (multiple choice, checklist, short answer, etc.). As students submitted their responses, the results were immediately organized into a spreadsheet, which allowed me to manipulate the data and really dig into the feedback my students were giving me. These surveys were anonymous, and students were able to not only evaluate our current library services, but also provide suggestions and recommendations for the future. As educators, it's important for us to solicit feedback from our students to assess our own practice, and Forms is the perfect tool to make this happen.

Working with colleagues using Drive is so simple and convenient. Teachers are able to share lesson plans, presentations, activity instructions, and assessments and work on them simultaneously, whether they're in the same room, different parts of the building, or even at home. For me, Drive makes collaborating on projects with fellow educators from around the world possible. I have presented webinars and conference sessions with librarians from completely opposite sides of the country. Using Google Drive, we are able to work together to create our presentation slides, plan our sessions, and give and receive feedback as we plan.

We've only recently acquired Drive accounts for our students, but the possibilities of collaboration are exciting. Students are able to easily access their files from home, which was a major issue when their files were hosted on the school's server. Students are also able to work collaboratively with classmates and receive instant feedback from teachers while they are working on their documents. Google Drive integrates nicely with Schoology, our school's learning management system, making it easy for students to access, edit, and submit their work.

A Student's View

From Chloe R., Grade 9:

I like Google Drive because I can start an assignment at school and if I don't finish—I can go home, log into Google Drive and I have my assignment. I also don't have the problem of not having the newest software update. Google Drive is always up to date!

Why Use Google Drive?

Google Drive can truly become the center of your Cloud classroom. With an immense storage capacity, it is an effective way for teachers and students to store important classroom files online. The ability to upload and create a variety of files gives you lots of options for working in the Cloud. Mix in a few different applications and you can do even more with your drive. Finally, Google Drive has solved the issues of collaborating in groups for teachers and students alike. Google Drive should be your classroom's home in the Cloud!

Taking It to a Higher Level

• Organize your files in Google Drive by creating folders. Then you can drag and drop files straight into the folders. This is an easy way to keep things tidy. Also, when you share a folder with others the files inside automatically receive the same permissions. Great for sharing an entire collection of documents all at once.

• Convert your files to the Google format. To help manage your storage in Google Drive be sure to convert your Office files to the corresponding Google file type. Found in the Settings menu, simply click the box that turns on the converting tool. This means that any Office file will automatically convert to Google Docs, Sheets, or Slides. Why would you do this? Google files are editable online in Google Drive while Office files upload as read only. Plus, Office files count against your overall storage, while Google files don't. To convert an Office file that has already been upload to Google Drive right click on the file and choose Open With. Then click on the Google version of the tool. It will create a Google file from your Office document.

- An effective tip for managing students in small groups is to use the See Revision History under the file menu in Google Docs, Sheets, and Slides. When the revision history launches, it allows the instructor to see all the changes to any project in Google Drive. Each student's work is highlighted and time stamped, thus giving the teacher the ability to quickly evaluate the contributions of each student. What a great way to manage student projects!

EVERNOTE

Bird's Eye View: Five Things to Know About Evernote

1. Evernote is a free service, but there is a premium option that costs $5/month or $45/year.

2. Free users get 60 MB of upload space each month with unlimited storage.

3. An individual note can hold up to 25 MB of data on a free account.

4. Free and Premium accounts can create up to 100,000 notes.

5. A user can create up to 250 notebooks.

What Is Evernote?

Evernote is a Cloud-based note-taking program that is designed to help users "Remember Everything." Using a system of notebooks and notes, users can store any information they want to recall. Users can post text notes, photos,

Source: @Evernote 2015

voice memos, and more in their notes. Evernote is a web-based and mobile accessible tool that allows users to access their information anywhere they are as long as they are connected to the Internet. When access is not available, new notes can still be created and will be synced when the device is reconnected to the Internet.

Evernote Features

Anywhere and Anytime

One of the great parts about Evernote is that it is device neutral. They have apps on all major mobile device platforms, and it can be accessed using any web browser. This allows all users the opportunity to access Evernote anywhere there is Internet access. Better yet, users using different devices can still share notes and notebooks with other users regardless of the device they are using. This is perfect for classrooms and districts that support the BYOD (bring your own device) model. With Evernote, teachers can share notes with their students without worrying about students having the correct device at home.

Bells and Whistles

Evernote has many great features that make note taking easy for all its users.

Reminders. A daily reminder can be set for each note that will send the user a notification on their mobile device to look at the note. This is perfect for the users who want to create notes as a way to remember to accomplish various tasks throughout the day.

Checkbox. Little checkboxes can be added to notes for those who like to check off their to-do lists as they go. They also are perfect for students to use to check of parts of an assignment they are completing for class.

Attachments. Users can attach files up to 25 MB. This can be a PowerPoint, PDF, JPEG, and other files users want to access.

Grids. Users can create different sized grids to help better organize information on the note. These can be used to help sort work to do on various days or to create rubrics for assignments.

Voice Memo. On mobile devices, users can create voice memos when typing is not convenient. This part of Evernote could be utilized to leave feedback to students on assignments in shared notebooks or notes.

Tags. Each note can be tagged with up to 100 individual tags to help sort information for later use. Tagging notes by assignment type (Essay, Project, etc.) can help the teacher see different assignments in different notebooks on different lessons.

Work Chat. Work Chat allows users to connect with others on notes and notebooks and share messages. It allows collaboration on Evernote work to go to the next level.

Down in the Trenches

Bec Spink is a teacher in Australia who uses Evernote as a way to engage her students in the classroom. She is an Evernote Ambassador and has been using Evernote for many years. Let's hear her story:

Being able to be prepared and have all lesson resources easily accessible and organised in advance is one of my favourite reasons why Evernote is so useful in the classroom. Before teaching, I make sure that I create a note to allow me to deliver content to students. To do this, I use Presentation mode. I love how Presentation mode creates a clean screen—no distractions or menus visible—students are able to focus on exactly what I want them to. As I move around my school a lot (I don't have my own class, or any one class that I work with regularly), I share notes with students by creating QR codes with the public link feature. As students enter the classroom, the QR code is displayed on a screen or IWB in an Evernote note. Students can then access lesson resources almost instantly, they save the note to their own account to make notes about the lesson or complete any tasks. This works for whole class (http://bit.ly/1MRPiCV) and small group (http://bit.ly/1ebp42F) situations.

Students in Years 5 and 6 at ACPS receive their homework via a blog (http://acps56homeworkblog.global2.vic.edu.au/), which was created by students in a Challenge Based Learning unit in 2013 and has carried on. At ACPS, homework is not compulsory; however, it was great to see this year that many students took it upon themselves to complete the homework in Evernote and share it with their teachers—this was done at students own accord, at the delight of one of their teachers.

During a writing lesson (https://www.evernote.com/shard/s122/share/9936-s122/#st=p&n=3eae2ae9-6d16-4091-94c8-8a3595c8e0a1) students were identifying how authors used imagery to describe settings. The used Evernote in-app Skitch annotation to highlight writing excerpts to describe sensory details in the writing.

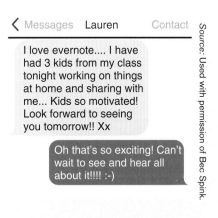

Source: Used with permission of Bec Spink.

The best part of students saving these lesson resources and their work to Evernote is when it comes to them doing their own writing or reading or need to refer back to a maths concept (http://bit.ly/1QVszGA) or lesson, they know they have saved it in Evernote

(Continued)

(Continued)

and it can be found and used easily. They don't have to waste time searching through their class books; it is instantly ready for them. This allows them to be far more independent in the classroom, they do not need to constantly ask so many questions—they are taking initiative, and they remember and can check what they have already done.

Most students have their accounts organised with different notebooks for subjects—they also have a portfolio notebook that they share with their teacher and parents. I like this transparency; in the past I have found that students in their later years of primary school rarely explain to their parents anything they do at school. Sharing notebooks with parents allows them to check in or stay informed about their child's progress. Come time for parent teacher interviews and three-way conferences, students, teachers, and parents are organised and have many discussion points that have arisen from the work already shared in Evernote.

Imagery Writing Lesson Plan (http://bit.ly/evernotelesson)

Learning Intention

We are learning to add descriptive details in writing so we can create an image in the reader's mind.

Success Criteria

We will be able to

- Read like a writer
- Identify words and phrases that appeal to senses
- Explain how descriptive language helps readers visualise

Australian Curriculum Link (http://bit.ly/austrcurr)

English / Year 6 / Literature / Examining literature

Content description

Identify the relationship between words, sounds, imagery and language patterns in narratives and poetry such as ballads, limericks and free verse

---

Elaborations

- identifying how language choice and imagery build emotional connection and engagement with the story or theme
- describing how a character's experience expressed through a verse novel impacts on students personally, how the author controls the revelation of the experiences and how the verse story builds meaning to its climax when we understand the whole

Source: ACARA (Australian Curriculum, Assessment and Reporting Authority)

English / Year 6 / Literature / Creating literature

Content description

Experiment with text structures and language features and their effects in creating literary texts, for example, using imagery, sentence variation, metaphor and word choice

---

Elaborations

- selecting and using sensory language to convey a vivid picture of places, feelings and events in a semi-structured verse form

---

Source: ACARA (Australian Curriculum, Assessment and Reporting Authority)

Whole Class Focus

Introduce the term. "Read like a writer." Discuss what this means.

Ask. How do authors use imagery to shape their writing?

Discuss responses. Students add ideas to Padlet (http://padlet.com/rebecca_spink/56 Bimagery).

Come up with a class definition of what sensory details are.

Model reading a text (e.g., see http://bit.ly/1QLkR1C) thinking aloud to visualise and make connections. Identify sensory details within the text. Foster discussion by asking

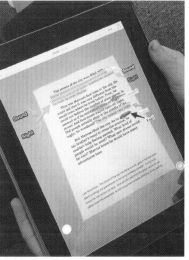

Source: ©Bec Spink 2014

What are the benefits of using sensory details in writing?

(Continued)

(Continued)

the following question: **Which words and phrases from the excerpts specifically appeal to a sense?** Annotate in Evernote using Skitch. As a class, identify the setting and list the words and phrases that describe touch, sounds, taste, smell, and sight underneath the picture.

Source: ©Bec Spink 2014

Student Independent Practice

Students investigate writing excerpts around the room. Students read the text as a "writer" and using Skitch in Evernote, annotate the sensory details in the text that create imagery. Students identify the setting and list the words and phrases that describe the senses.

Source: Used with permission of Bec Spink.

Reflection

Refer back to Padlet (http://padlet.com/rebecca_spink/56Bimagery) and add any more ideas and details. Discuss, share excerpts and good examples students located.

Bec Spink

eLearning Leading Teacher

Aitken Creek Primary School

Melbourne, Australia

Twitter: @missb6_2

Website: becspink.com

Assessment

Evernote Work sample, Padlet responses

A Student's View

From Alessandra, 9 years old, Year 5:

I like Evernote because it is organised and I can easily find my notes, when I am reading I have my notes all in one spot, not scattered all over the place.

From Anthymus, 11 years old, Year 6:

> I like Evernote because it keeps my work organised, I never lose my work because it is in the Cloud and you can actually read my writing.

From Caroline C., Grade 10:

> Using Evernote in English Class has been the biggest life-saver of the school year. It is so nice not having to worry about where I can find my notes, assignments, homework, etc. Having everything in one place that is accessible from anywhere just by a click of a button has saved me so much time and has kept me so much more organized.

From Louise B., Grade 10:

> Evernote makes being a student much easier. The fact that I can access all of my notes from class while on my phone makes me more productive and a better student. If I need to study, I can quickly pull up the note on my phone. If I have an idea for an upcoming assignment, I can easily put it down with all of my other information.

Why Use Evernote?

Evernote is the perfect solution for people looking to take notes and have access to them whenever they want, wherever they want. Evernote allows users to store photos, PDFs, and much more to make organizing information easier for everyone. For teachers, Evernote can be used for lesson planning because it can keep all assignments and the day-to-day work they want to have access to on the go. For students, Evernote is perfect because they no longer have to worry about carrying around many different notebooks from class to class because all their notes and notebooks can be found on their personal device in the pocket. Evernote is perfect for schools that are using the BYOD model because it works across all platforms, so there is no worry about downloading software for students and their parents. Evernote stores all the user's information in the Cloud, and users can pull it down when the need it. Evernote's goal is to help people "Remember Everything," and that is exactly what students and teachers need.

Taking It to a Higher Level

• Creating shared notebooks that hold all the assigned work from class will allow students to join and have access to the assignments from their personal devices. Also, parents can join these notebooks and have access to the work to help their students stay on task during the school year.

• Teachers can set reminders on all the assignment notes so they and students who have joined that notebook will also receive the reminder notification on their personal device.

• Slides from class presentations can be saved in Evernote notes in shared notebooks so all students can access them and review them later in the year.

2

Communicating
in the Cloud

Communication has changed with all the exciting new tools available. It is important for educators, parents, and students to take advantage of these tools. Remind, Google Hangouts, Voxer, and many others have allowed people to go more in-depth with their communication to better support learning. This learning can be for the students and the educator. There are some valid concerns when it comes to communication in the Cloud, but tech companies are working hard to make sure that all users have their privacy protected so communication can be quick and safe. Although there are some concerns with communicating in the Cloud, these tools should be used by all education stakeholders to take their schools to the next level.

Privacy has always been a concern when it comes to technology. From the biggest companies to the smallest start-ups, privacy is something that everyone needs to take seriously. While there have been security breaches in the past, these issues have been addressed and safety measures have been put in place to protect user information. The battle between hackers and companies will be ongoing, but that is no reason to avoid using Cloud-based technology for communication. With the correct safety precautions, Cloud-based tools can be used safely with parents, teachers, and students.

It is always important for teachers to fully investigate any tool they are going to use in the classroom and pay close attention to the information they are requesting. It is important to keep personal accounts separate from school accounts. Create special accounts that will only be used for school connections and lessons. This will prevent any personal information from appearing in class in front of students. It is also important to check a building's or district's rules regarding student interaction with web-based programs. Every district has a different set of rules, so it is always important to be in compliance. Last, it is important for teachers to communicate to parents that the classroom will be using Cloud-based technology to communicate with others outside the classroom. The parents might have questions about the safety of such connections, so it is important for the teacher to do all the research and share with the parents all the wonderful positive experiences that can be had when students are connected. There are many reasons to use these great tools, and here are a few to help any educator get started.

In the past, getting information to students and parents was not very easy after the school day. Unless phone calls were going to be placed to every single home, it would be next to impossible to share new and important information with these students and parents. Cloud-based communication tools now allow communication to anyone at any time. The Remind app allows users to sign up for text message reminders. A teacher can create a class for students and parents to join and assignment reminders can be shared after school. If there is a change in the schedule, a message can be shared quickly to let parents and students know so they can be prepared. Remind also allows the teachers to attach documents, so permission slips and other important forms can be sent via text so nothing is lost or forgotten.

Evernote allows users to create shared notebooks where notes can be created and viewed by anyone granted access to these notebooks. By placing new notes in these shared notebooks, students can stay up-to-date on the homework given in class. Having these notes available to students allows them more access to the information and increases the likelihood that they will complete the assignment or submit the correct form. The ability to create and share messages quickly allows teachers to communicate more effectively with their classes. Evernote also allows users to set notification reminders, so parents and students can be notified on the go. There are other great ways to communicate in the Cloud that go beyond just sending messages.

Video conferencing is a tool that is straight out of science fiction. The ability to make video calls seemed like a dream, but it is now a reality and an important part of Cloud-based communication. Skype is a great tool that allows users to have a video call. As long as the users are connected to an Internet connection, people can talk face-to-face. For some, having a conversation where they can actually see the person is very important to them. If Skype is on the user's phone, the user can give tours of a house during a conversation or present student work as well. The ability to be mobile and have a video conversation opens up many exciting possibilities for all users. If a parent cannot make it to Parent/Teacher night, a Skype conversation could be the perfect solution for the teacher to consider so the valuable meeting can still be held. If students are sick at home, a Skype call into the class could allow the students to be part of class, even if they are not there. Skype is not the only tool that is perfect for video conferencing. Google offers a great tool that allows for video conversations and whole lot more.

Google Hangouts takes the video call and ramps it up for the users. Having a conversation with multiple people can be great, but sometimes work needs to take place at the same time. Instead of bouncing between multiple screens, Google Hangouts allow users to work on a document at the same time. This really takes communication and collaboration and throws them together. They truly make a great pair. This type of communication and collaboration is so important for teachers and students. Here is what teacher Amanda C. Dykes said about it:

> It can be real-time collaboration or on your own time collaboration. Sometimes I like to collaborate at that moment but often I can't because of work or kids. So I'm glad I can input when it's convenient. (personal communication, September 20, 2014)

The part that is really important to note is the "real-time collaboration." Sending a one-way communication using Cloud tools can be helpful, but meeting a student via video to help them through an essay can be invaluable to them. That real-time connection can help a struggling student avoid serious mistakes by answering a few questions. Some teachers will even hold office hours online for students or parents who have some questions. The lives of students have become much busier, so their questions might not arise until later in the day after multiple extracurricular activities. Cloud-based communication tools allow teachers to be available with a very flexible schedule. Skype and Google Hangouts are available on mobile devices, so educators can even take meetings on the go. These options allow educators to really make a difference with students and address minor issues before they become serious problems. With great communication, students can accomplish anything. These Cloud-based tools also knock down the walls of the classroom and open up the world to them.

Principal Amber Teamann had this to say about why she loves communicating in the Cloud: "It's the ability to connect asynchronously with people around the world." This is such a key point when it comes to communicating in the Cloud. In the past, classrooms were very limited in how they could connect their class with others from around the world. The pen pal has been a staple of the classroom for decades, but that has now evolved. No longer do students need to wait weeks for letters to traverse the country or cross the ocean; instead, connections can be made quickly using blogs. The same messages can be shared on a blog, and they do not have to be sent around the world. The interactions can be very quick and allow for near instant feedback. Students can share a post with their readers and see the response on the very next day. Better yet, the students can keep these conversations going at home long after school hours have ended. By using blogging as a communication tool, students no longer have to wait for school to keep connected with their new friends from all over the world. Sharing these blogs has gotten even easier with the use of Twitter in the classroom.

Twitter has been great for communicating in the Cloud. Besides the ability to quickly share information in 140 characters or less, Twitter can be used to make connections that can extend beyond a single tweet. The hashtag #Comments4Kids is used by educators all over the world to share the work their students are doing with the educational community. By using this hashtag, students will have a global audience for their blogs instead of the audience of one, their teacher, which they are used to having for writing assignments. Director of Technology Michelle Triemstra said,

> Cloud-based tools provide easy access to information regardless of the time zone or geographic location. In an educational setting, they provide students with the ability to communicate with each other beyond their physical classroom and create a classroom without walls. (personal communication, September 20, 2014)

Twitter is a wonderful tool that allows educators to make these connections for their students. It can be used to reach out to authors or experts who might be willing to have a Twitter conversation with a class or possibly have a video call so students can meet their favorite author virtually. These connections can have a profound impact on student learning and all it takes is a simple tweet.

Communication has never been easier. Using Cloud-based tools to communicate allows for real-time communication from anywhere at anytime. Teacher Jennifer Bond sums up Cloud-based communication best:

> Cloud-based tools allow me to communicate to my students, families, and PLN anytime, anywhere, and with any device! Creation, collaboration, and communication whether we are within our schools walls or beyond, making learning full of possibilities and connections continuous! (personal communication, September 20, 2014)

The great tools offer opportunities to educators, parents, and students to make education more accessible. When learning becomes less of a burden for students, they will be more engaged. Cloud-based tools allow educators to take traditional lessons and spice them by opening a world of possibilities to them. While there might be some concerns over privacy, there are far more positive reasons why educators should embrace Cloud-based communication for education.

TWITTER

Bird's Eye View: Five Things to Know About Twitter

1. Twitter can be used to create a personal class hashtag to collect student and teacher tweets over the course of the year.

2. Twitter can be used as a back channel during class discussion.

3. Photos and videos can be shared on Twitter so parents can see what is happening in class.

4. Teachers can live tweet field trips for parents and the community to share the experience.

5. Connect with other classrooms and share thoughts on shared curriculum.

What Is Twitter?

 Twitter is a microblogging site that allows users to post messages called tweets, which are limited to 140 characters, to followers. Nonregistered users can view public tweets by going to Twitter.com, and users with accounts can post tweets and connect with other users. Twitter allows users to post pictures and videos as well. In education, Twitter is used by educators to connect with others on various topics to share ideas and grow professionally. Twitter can also be used in various ways with students in the classroom to engage them in the learning process after the school day has ended.

Twitter Features

Tweet. The most basic use of Twitter is to send a message up to 140 characters long. This could include links or just a simple good morning to the world.

Hashtag. A hashtag (#) on Twitter is how users tag their tweets so they can be referenced by others who search that specific hashtag. #EdChat is used for teachers who are sharing ideas other educators might find interesting.

Photos. Twitter allows users to attach photos to their tweets and share with the world around them.

Video. Users are able to shoot and edit a video up to 30 seconds and share that on Twitter. This takes communication on Twitter to another level.

Direct Message. DMs are a way to send private messages to others Twitter users that will not be seen by the rest of Twitter world.

Group Direct Message. This newest feature now allows multiple people to be involved in a private direct message.

Let's Chat

Another great aspect of Twitter is the chats. Chats are designated times that educators get together to discuss specific topics for one hour. Here are some Twitter chats that are worth checking out: http://bit.ly/18mkQkw

#1to1Chat. This chat takes place on Sundays at 9PM EST and focuses on educators in a one-to-one environment.

#EngChat. This chat focuses on English Language Arts and takes place on Mondays at 7PM EST.

#EdChat. This is the first education chat, and it takes place on Tuesdays at 7PM EST. Topics are decided by a poll that goes out earlier in the week.

#MichEd. This chat is one of many state-organized chats and takes place on Wednesdays at 8PM EST. Nick can often be found participating in #MichEd.

#UTedChat. Another of the state education chats. This chat takes place weekly on Wednesday at 9PM MST. You'll find Jared participating in #UTedChat.

#MathChat. Math teachers unite to talk about numbers on Thursdays at 7PM EST.

#GTChat. This is a chat for teachers of gifted and talented students, and it takes place on Fridays at 7PM EST.

#SatChat. This chat focuses on general education questions for those who are up early with their coffee on Saturdays at 7:30AM EST.

There are many more chats that teachers can find and participate in. Better yet, any teacher can create their own hashtag chat to connect with like-minded educators.

Other Hashtags to Follow

#Comments4Kids. This is a tag that educators use to connect their student blogs to other educators who have their students' blogs as well. The idea is to create a large audience for the students and their ideas.

#GAFE. This hashtag is used for teachers who are using Google Apps for Education in their class and want to share resources and connect with other GAFE districts.

#PBL. This hashtag is used by teachers that are using Project Based Learning in their classroom.

#GeniusHour and #20Time. This hashtag is great for finding resources and other educators who are using Genius Hour and 20 Time in their classroom.

#EdTech. This is a great chat for looking up new tools that teachers could use in their classroom.

Down in the Trenches

Phillip Cummings, a sixth-grade teacher from Memphis, TN, uses Twitter in his classroom and has come up with an interesting lesson. Let's hear his story:

Chief Tweeting Officers*

I'm trying something new this year using Twitter in class. I've designated a Chief Tweeting Officer (CTO) role in my sixth-grade reading class. I created a class Twitter account, @MrCsClass, a couple of years ago, but I never really did much with it. Occasionally, I used it to share things my students were learning and doing in class, but it was always from my perspective and I used it very inconsistently. I want this year to be different. I want my students to have a greater voice, and I want us to share regularly. I hope our rotating CTO job will help us down that road.

Our school has a dedicated hashtag #PDSmem, and in my room we have a dedicated Twitter device, too. While at ISTE 2013 this summer I received a free Surface tablet that I wanted to integrate into our learning environment. Using the Surface allows me administrative control but gives the students the easy access they need. So far, I'm liking the way that it's working for us.

When introducing my classes to Twitter, I gave the students a handout at the beginning of class to use for Practice Tweets. We talked about what kinds of things people might want to know about our learning and how we might use Twitter to connect with learners around the world. We discussed including images, hashtags, and links and the importance of adding value to others with what we share. The students had to write two or three tweets during class time while we went about our other class activities. The handout had to be submitted back at the end of class as a "ticket out the door." On the next page is the handout I created (each space represents a character).

Phillip Cummings
Sixth-Grade Reading Teacher
Memphis, TN
Twitter: @Phillip_Cummings
Website:
http://www.philipcummings.com/

*Used with permission from Phillip Cummings' blog: http://www.philipcummings.com/chief-tweeting-officers/

(Continued)

(Continued)

Practice Tweets

Write a good "headline" tweet for today's class.

— —
— —
— —
— —

Write a "deep question" tweet that you have about today's class.

— —
— —
— —
— —

Write a "highlight" tweet for today's learning.

— —
— —
— —
— —

Write a "connection" tweet tying our learning with something outside our class.

— —
— —
— —
— —

Create you own original tweet about something related to our learning.

— —
— —
— —
— —

Make sure to include our school hashtag, other related hashtags, and your initials at the end of your tweet. An ideal tweet is under 120 characters. This allows room for others to retweet and comment.

Source: ©Phillip Cummings 2014

(Next time, I might have students send their tweets through a Google form, but for this first exercise I wanted them to use the hashed lines to see the number of characters available.)

I took my class rosters and have assigned students different days where they will serve as our CTO (Chief Tweeting Officer). When the CTO enters the room, he picks up the Surface tablet so he can tweet a few times during the class period. We've only been at it a few days, but the boys have done a good job so far. Following is a sample of some of their tweets.

Mr. Cummings' Class
@MrCsClass   Follow

Today we learned that we are like something that we all had no idea we were like. We created #bridges about ourselves. #PDSmem /RW

5:06 PM - 19 Aug 2013

1 RETWEET

 Mr. Cummings' Class
@MrCsClass   Follow

Today we did a See, Think, Wonder to show the differences between Poland and Denmark during the Nazi attack. #pdsmem / SDK

3:21 PM - 29 Aug 2013

1 RETWEET

 Mr. Cummings' Class
@MrCsClass   Follow
Posting our first blog post on kidblog. bit.ly/6B2013 #PDSmem /GC

9:59 AM - 4 Sep 2013

3 RETWEETS

 Mr. Cummings' Class
@MrCsClass   Follow

Today in class we are doing the ladder of feedback and what to do to have a good ladder of feedback. #pdsmem /ab

2:23 PM - 6 Sep 2013

Source: Tweets used with permission of Phillip Cummings.

(Continued)

(Continued)

As I said, it's a good start. Hopefully, as the semester goes we'll be able to connect with some other learners and other classes. We'd love to make some global connections and develop some friendships around the world as we go.

Real Time Gatsby

Another creative way to use Twitter is to create accounts based on novels that are being covered in class. I created an account and live tweeted the story *The Great Gatsby* as the students were reading. Here are some examples of the tweets.

I was able to have some fun and engage the students in discussions about the characters and their actions after they read the tweets and came to class. Twitter was a great way to share some of the funnier aspects of the story and take a different approach to introducing themes and symbols.

Students had a fun time engaging with the account and wanted to create their own tweets for the characters. They shared them in class, and we discussed how accurate the tweets were and why the characters might feel that way. Twitter allowed the students to connect with a story in a different way and bring class discussion to a different level.

A Student's View

From Halle M., Grade 10:

Twitter makes it easy to be connected with the class. It is helpful to be able to see my homework on my Twitter feed. If I ever have a question, it is easy and quick to get a hold of Mr. Provenzano by just sending him a tweet.

Why Use Twitter?

Twitter is a great tool that allows educators to connect with others from all over the world. While only limited to 140 characters, great conversations and connections can start on Twitter and lead to deeper conversations through e-mail or video chats. Teachers can search for their own professional development whenever and wherever they are. No longer do teachers need to search Google for the best answers to their educational problems because the experts are on Twitter and they are willing to share and connect with all educators who join the conversation. There is a saying that the smartest person in the room is the room, and that is exactly what Twitter can be for educators.

Taking It to a Higher Level

- If your students are too young to create Twitter accounts, have them create paper tweets that can be posted to a bulletin board. These tweets can be about what they had learned for the day or just how they are feeling at the start of school.

- Reach out to authors of popular novels and have students ask them questions about their favorite characters and events.

- Have students engage in conversations with politicians and ask them questions regarding current events.

REMIND

Bird's Eye View: Five Things to Know About Remind

1. Remind is a text messaging system between teachers, students, and parents.

2. No personal contact information, such as phone numbers or e-mail addresses, is shared between teachers, students, and parents.

3. Remind is a free app on Android and iOS.

4. Teachers can send photos, documents, presentations, voice clips, or PDFs.

5. Texts can be set up in advance for later dates.

What Is Remind?

Source: @remind 2015

Communication is key in the classroom, but getting in contact with today's students is harder than ever. They are on the go from one activity to the next, and e-mail is not an efficient way to connect. Parents are just as busy as students, and they want to stay in the loop as well. Remind has created a safe and easy tool for teachers to use that allows for quick and easy communication with students and parents to keep them informed of the daily classroom events.

Remind is a free tool that allows teachers to send mass text messages without having to access students' private cell phone numbers and without the students having access to the teacher's phone number. It has already been adopted by 35 percent of the K–12 teacher population in the United States.

Teachers create a Remind account and share the access code with students and parents. The students and parents text the access code to the number provided by Remind for the teacher and they have now joined the class. After joining the class, they will be able to receive information from the teacher through safe text messages. The messages shared on Remind cannot be edited or deleted, and an entire downloadable message history is available to each teacher. The ability to quickly and easily send information is crucial in today's fast-paced world, and Remind has found a perfect way to do that while keeping the privacy of its users intact.

Remind can be accessed through a web browser or through a free app on Android and iOS devices. Multiple classes can be created and can be added to one text to save teachers time when communicating with multiple classes that need the same information. Text feeds for specific classes can also be embedded on websites for viewing by those who might not have access to text messages.

Remind Features

Remind did not stop at just sending text messages to others. Remind allows users to send various attachments through text message as well.

Photos. Sending photos to a class and parents is a great way to share the everyday aspects of the classroom. Field trip photos, project photos, and anything teachers want to share visually from their classroom can now be safely texted to an entire class.

Voice Clips. When a picture and some words are not enough, Remind allows for teachers to send voice clips. Tone can play a big part in sending messages, so a voice clip can ensure that the message is received in the way the teacher intended. It's just another tool in making communication stronger between students, parents, and teachers.

Documents and PDFs. Sometimes it is important to make sure that certain documents get home or to the students. These could be permission slips or study guides. Too often students lose these important items and miss out. By sending a text message to parents and students, everyone can have all the documents they need in a digital format. It is a wonderful way to create a paperless system in the classroom as well.

Presentations. There are times when students want to see the presentation that was shared in class by the teacher. An easy way to do that now is to send it directly to the students' phones. They can now review the presentation on their mobile devices any time they want. By having more access to the information, the students can be better prepared for class.

Stamps. Stamps are a great way for students to respond to messages sent by the teacher without having a full conversation. Students can

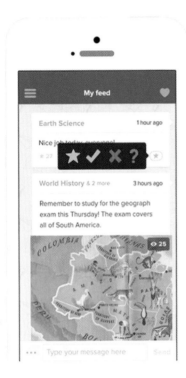

Source: @remind 2015

respond with a check mark, star, question mark, or an X to let the teacher know what they are thinking in response to the Remind that was just sent to them. This is an excellent way to have some communication back and forth without opening the door to full conversations.

Chat

There will be times when one-to-one communication will be necessary, and Remind has this covered. With this new feature, two-way communication is easier and safer than ever. Students might have a specific problem with an assignment and need to reach out to their teacher, or a parent might have questions about an upcoming field trip or conference night. What makes two-way communication safe on Remind is that no personal contact info is shared, and messages can't be deleted or edited (everyone will have access to transcript history). Chat is a new feature that has not been released by publication time, but we highly encourage you to visit Remind.com or download the app to check out this cool tool that can allow you to take communication with students and parents to the next level.

All these options demonstrate how easy it is to connect with students and parents outside the classroom. Sometimes students are out sick, have a dental appointment, are at a sporting event, or some other reason that takes them out of the class. Instead of having students or parents search through a website or sending the teacher an e-mail, they can just wait for a text message from their teacher that will have everything they need.

Down in the Trenches

Brian S. Friedlander, PhD, is an education professor and has seen the value of using Remind with his students. He sees it as a great way to enhance communication with the students in his class. Let's hear his story:

When I first learned about Remind, I was really excited with all the possibilities, but when I finally got to use it in class, I learned what a powerful tool it was! As a professor of education, I teach both under- graduate and graduate students courses in assistive technology, and while I have access to e-mail, many of my students today are so inundated with e-mail that it gets lost in the fray. Having access to a text messaging service like Remind has been a godsend. If you are not familiar with Remind, it allows teachers to use their cell phones or computers to send out text messages to students at no cost. The text messages are uploaded to a server that prevents recipients from replying, thus eliminating the need for teachers to give out their personal cell phone numbers. Being able to quickly shoot off a text message to my students that I know they will attend to is extremely important and has worked like a charm for me ever since I started to use it.

At the beginning of each semester during the first session of class, I have the students sign up for the Remind text messaging service. With each update, Remind has made it even easier for students to sign up for the service and in a matter of minutes all my students are signed on to the service. Remind was critical to me during Hurricane Sandy and helped me stay in touch with my students when all other means of communication were down. As soon as I heard any informa- tion from the college, I was able to push out a text message to keep my students informed. Because text messages require such small bandwidth, text messages often can go through when other means of communication fail. For the past 2 years, I have used Remind suc- cessfully with students in my class to remind them of important due dates and appointments. Just recently, Remind has allowed teachers to text message small groups (three students as a minimum) that are within the class. This has proved to be a great tool for me when I am setting up mentoring and advising with my students. On the day of the meeting, I can quickly text only those students who have meet- ings with me in the late afternoon. If I want, I can even schedule these text messages ahead of time to be delivered on a certain date, which has worked really well. Now that Remind allows teachers to attach files to a text message, I can think of some new and creative ways to use this in my classroom. Remind is indispensable to me as a pro- fessor and one that allows me to quickly get my students' attention

(Continued)

(Continued)

to remind them of important events. I would highly recommend that teachers take a look at Remind, which is a great tool to communicate with your students.

Brian S. Friedlander, PhD

Associate Professor of Education at the College of St. Elizabeth

Morristown, NJ

Twitter: @assistivetek

Website: http://assistivetek.blogspot.com

A Student's View

From Nathan B., Grade 10:

> If you are someone who doesn't use planners, this is a lifesaver!

From Alexander B., Grade 10:

> Most of my teachers will send out reminders about homework before school gets out, so it's easy to remember what I need to bring home.

Why Use Remind?

Remind creates a safe and open way to communicate to students and parents efficiently to keep everyone informed of what is happening in the classroom. In the mobile world, it is important to meet people where they are, and Remind offers a wonderful application that allows educators to do that. Best of all, it is a free service that utilizes devices that are already in the hands of the users.

Taking It to a Higher Level

There are other uses for Remind in the school system that should be considered:

• **School Clubs.** Sometimes these groups do not meet very often, so communication in keeping everyone on the same page is important. All permission slips and meeting notes can be shared with members who could not attend a meeting.

- **Sports Teams.** Coaches can quickly send messages to players and parents if there is a change in the practice schedule or game time. Instead of having to enter all the numbers in every time there is a change, a simple text to one group can be made.

- **Administration.** Remind would be a great tool for administrators to keep in quick communication with different groups of staff members. Groups can be created based on departments, custodial groups, and other parts of the school for quick messages and the sharing of important documents. School closings could be quickly shared to entire buildings with just a few simple texts to groups.

GOOGLE HANGOUTS

Bird's Eye View: Five Things to Know About Google Hangouts

1. Google Hangouts allow video conferencing for up to 10 people.

2. Hangouts can be scheduled, broadcast, and recorded as part of the Hangouts on Air feature.

3. Beyond video conferencing, Google Hangouts can also incorporate streamed YouTube video, Google Drive, Fun Effects, and Screensharing.

4. Hangouts can be accessed on mobile devices, tablets, desktops, and laptops.

5. Instant messaging in Hangouts can include text, images, animated gifs, and more.

What Is Google Hangouts?

Communication for teachers and students has undergone a dramatic shift in the Internet age. Where classrooms would have previously created relationships through written correspondence like pen pals, now everything has gone to video. The ability to have live video conferencing gives classrooms a convenient way to learn from teachers and students from anywhere in the world. Google Hangouts is your tool to facilitate communicating in the Cloud.

Google Hangouts allows you to create an online video conference call between you and up to nine other people. The Hangouts are facilitated through Gmail contacts so you'll want to be sure you share contact information before the call. To initiate a call, you can select a contact in your Gmail and click on the video camera icon ▦. Immediately a call will be initiated and, when the other party answers the call, you'll enter a private video conference call.

Google Hangouts are available from most devices with an Internet connection. This provides teachers and students incredible flexibility because they can participate in the video chat regardless of which device they have in their hands. In fact, Hangouts can start on a mobile device and switch to a laptop when the student gets in front of the computer.

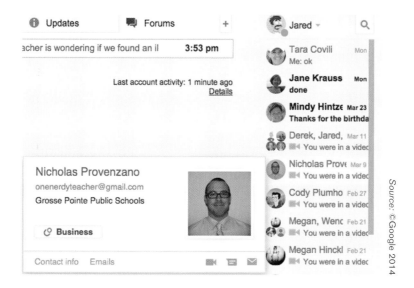

Google Hangouts Features for the Classroom

You can enable your Google Hangouts with many different features to enhance your video chats and bring collaboration to a whole new level.

Live Chat. In addition to your video feed, use the chat feature to share links, images, and back channel discussions in the sidebar. This is a great way to moderate a panel discussion with your students.

Screenshare. Switch from the video camera to display the computer screen and share information with your audience. With screenshare you can do a live presentation from your computer, share websites, navigate through classroom assignments, and more.

Google Drive. Enable Google Drive in your Hangout and share documents with your audience. This will allow the members of your Hangout to collaborate in real time, while having a conversation about the document using microphones.

Remote Desktop. Allows you to get help from someone in your contacts. They can take over your screen and provide you with

the assistance you need. You can also enter Remote Desktop to provide help for others.

Hangouts on Air

One of the best features of Google Hangouts is the ability to manage the video conference using Hangouts On Air. Google allows users to schedule a Hangout for a future time and then invite their guests to attend. Hangouts On Air can be broadcast from your YouTube Channel or Google+ channel, or you can embed the Hangout into your own website.

The other major feature of Hangout On Air is the ability to record the presentations for archiving purposes. Imagine saving the guest lecture or panel discussion so your students can go back and review the materials later. This is perfect for those students who were absent on the day of the Hangout, either due to illness or other circumstances. Hangout can have a recording time of up to several hours so you can feel confident in using this tool for archiving a variety of video chats.

Down in the Trenches

Tricia Fuglestad from Arlington Heights, IL, has been using Google Hangouts as part of her professional development trainings. Here is her story:

> Google Hangouts have been an essential element of my professional life because I have been traveling around Illinois and parts of Indiana this school year to conduct iPad professional development workshops for art teachers. When I lead teachers through the steps of creating a piece of art, the lesson is paced to the needs of the learners. I stop, answer questions, give examples, and demonstrate as we work together.
>
> In November, I was asked by Susan Riley of Education Closet to try to conduct an hour-long iPad workshop via Google Hangouts to a live audience of over 55 teachers from around the country. This was a synchronous event where attendees could text in questions that I would respond to during the last 15 minutes. I shared my screen and did a tutorial for 45 minutes looking at eight different iPad art lessons each exploring different techniques. I stopped screen share and answered questions from the chat window then signed off after an hour.

The following video was recorded in my YouTube account and archived for others to watch at whatever pace they wished. Here is the link: educationcloset.com/creating-ipads-master-class.

This model would work well with a room full of workshop attendees in a location that would be either too expensive to physically attend or too disruptive for my own art students for me to be absent. I think that Google Hangouts could create a feeling of being in the room if I could have two-way conversations, which I know is possible. This could very easily make meaningful PD much more affordable.

Source: Used with permission of Tricia Fuglestad.

Tricia Fuglestad

K–5 Elementary Teacher

Dryden Elementary School

Arlington Heights, IL

Twitter: @Fuglefun

Website: http://drydenart .weebly.com/fugleblog.html

Another educator using Google Hangouts On Air is Jeff McCauley from Kaysville, UT. Jeff teaches marketing at the high school level, and Hangouts has provided his students with an amazing experience of connecting with various business leaders.

Google+ Hangouts are perhaps the most powerful tool to come along in education since I began teaching over 30 years ago. I know, that's a strong statement, but I believe it's true.

For the past couple of years I've had several experiences with Google+ Hangouts that have allowed my students to gain insight and information from industry professionals that would not have been available before this technology.

It began a few years back when we were able to secure a Hangout with Daymond John of *Shark Tank* fame. Google was interested in using this Hangout as an example of how education could use the technology. They were actively involved, and the event was only the fourth time the Hangout On Air (HOA) option was used. It was not even offered to the public at this time. We were really on the leading edge.

(Continued)

(Continued)

As for the value of the Hangout, as you might expect with his credibility and celebrity status, the students hung on every word. As a teacher, it was a little frustrating, knowing I could've said the exact same words, but I lacked the credibility. But the truth is, instead of fighting it, we need to take advantage of it.

Another draw to this particular event is the fact that we invited schools from across the country to join the Hangout. Many struggled because the technology was relatively new. Now, it's second nature for many teachers.

Over the next few years, my students were able to sit in on a variety of Google Hangouts. This group included individuals from the business world, peace sports business world, and in the social media marketing world.

While most Hangouts were simply a 30-minute portion of the class, there were two instances that went far beyond that. On two separate occasions we literally had an entire daylong series of Hangouts. One was focused on sports marketing, and the other on social media marketing. While I don't recommend an entire day for the faint of heart, it was a pretty exciting experience.

I am often asked how I am able to contact individuals willing to participate in a Hangout. I look to find people I think my students would like to hear from; then, I try to contact them. While I'm certainly not successful at each effort, you'd be surprised at how willing people are to help out, particularly when the requirements are so minimal.

The method of contacting may vary from person to person, but I have found that social media is perhaps most effective. On one occasion I was looking over my Twitter feed during my prep period. I read a tweet from an industry expert inviting people to join his live presentation. Since I had the time, I checked it out for a few minutes. I then tweeted a comment about his presentation, and he followed by favoring the tweet.

When he favorited the tweet, I knew he was paying attention, so I tweeted back and asked if he wanted to share his thoughts with a group of high school students in a Hangout. His response was a name of a contact person, and we quickly arranged the details. Keep in mind that this author and speaker is paid thousands of dollars to travel the world and make presentations.

I have developed a list of marketing and business teachers interested in participating in Hangouts. As a result, each time I arrange for a Hangout, I make sure to invite them. Obviously, very few can join us live. That is what I like about the HOA option. Teachers and/or students are able to go to my YouTube page and watch the presentations at their convenience.

Source: Used with permission of Jeff McCauley.

Jeff McCauley

Marketing Teacher

Davis High School

Layton, UT

Twitter: @jeffmccauley

Website/blog: TheMarketingTeacher.com

Recommended Tools to Explore: Symbaloo, DropItToMe, buzzspice, Wix.com

Regardless of what subject you teach, there is a role for G+ HOA to play. While there are countless uses for Hangouts in education, my favorite is allowing my students to learn from the experts.

Here is my challenge. It is a simple one: have your first G+ HOA in the next 30 days. No excuses . . . just make it happen.

A Student's View

Sara S., an eleventh-grade student at Turkey Run High School in Indiana, shared her experience using Google Hangouts:

Using video chats in Spanish class was very helpful and interesting. Being able to practice and speak with other students from Spain was beneficial to both parties. We were able to practice and better our understanding of the languages we studied by having conversations and asking each other questions. We enjoyed the benefits of international travel and had cultural experiences without having to leave the classroom. We learned that the students in Spain were not that much different from us. We found out that we were all interested in the same topics.

Why Google Hangouts?

Google Hangouts is the go-to tool for video conferencing in the Cloud. Regardless of the device or platform, you can easily share with up to 10 of your colleagues or students. With built-in features for sharing, communicating, and presenting, Hangouts are a great way to learn from more than a talking head. Finally, Hangouts On Air provide teachers with the perfect option to broadcast and archive classroom videoconferences. Google Hangouts are a must have for every classroom teacher!

Taking It to a Higher Level

• Use Google Hangouts with students to create the Remote Study Group. Students won't need to meet at the library anymore. Just have the kids set a time, and they can work with one another from a variety of locations. Better yet, they can work collaboratively using the Google Docs plug-in to the Hangout.

• Schedule Google Hangouts as a part of Google Calendar events. In the details for your Google Calendar event you add a video call to be part of the event. This is a great way to get your Hangout set up and provide the members of the group easy access to the video chat.

• Create video tutorials. Using Hangouts, you can create step-by-step tutorials that can be saved using Hangouts On Air. Simply send your audience to the archived link and they can watch you share your screen in an online tutorial!

3

Collaborating in the Cloud

Our classrooms have changed. We are no longer able to work in isolation with individual students working at the desks with long periods of silent study. The Internet has brought the world together and turned physical barriers of school walls into information nets. Teachers are also finding the Cloud has helped them work with colleagues from schools across the globe. As Beth Campbell states,

> My life is easier in that I have 24/7 access to everything I create, store, and use. I can collaborate with others across the world. It has made me a stronger and more connected teacher. Isolation is not an option. (personal communication, January 5, 2014)

Students want to work with their classmates to explore content and create projects. The Cloud has provided students the opportunity to work with their classmates regardless of location. Now they can work on projects at anytime. Even the constraint of collaborating across time zones is less of a burden than ever before. Students can jump in and out of shared documents whenever they have a free moment.

Finally, the Cloud allows students the chance to collaborate regardless of device and platform. It doesn't matter whether students are using a desktop or mobile device. They can be on a Mac or PC—as long as there is an Internet connection, students can collaborate with one another.

Access, Not Attachments

One of the biggest changes brought about by the Cloud is the way in which information is exchanged. Collaboration used to require massive amounts of e-mail exchanging hands with file management becoming a nightmare. Now, students and teachers can share files by simply adding the collaborator's e-mail address. No more e-mail attachments, just one document stored online, with access for multiple people.

Tools like Google Docs make it easy to work on files with others. You can watch edits being made in real time, and students don't have to wait around to get access to the shared file. They can all work on the same document at the same time. Teachers can have class brainstorms where all the students can collaborate with one another.

Empowering Student Voices

Using Cloud tools for collaboration can bring new voices into classroom conversations. In the traditional classroom format, few students participate in a whole class discussion. Some are shy and don't want to draw attention to themselves. Others may feel pressure to come up with the right answer on the spot and need more time to reflect. Some know that if they can just wait it out, one or two students will always jump in to give the answers. By moving these conversations into online spaces, teachers provide students with the opportunity to participate without any of the social anxieties they may feel in class.

"Students who once sat in the back of the room and didn't want to speak up or be part of the lesson now are excited to get online and share what they're learning. They want to teach others and they feel like their voice matters," said Jill Barnes, a seventh-grade teacher at Grafton Middle School in York County, VA (Jackson, 2013).

Using Google Docs or Edmodo to have the entire class share thoughts in a brainstorm document or message board is a great way to have all students contribute their thoughts. In a one-to-one classroom, these activities can happen during instruction time, because students can use any Internet-ready device to make their contributions.

Learn From the World

Information has no bounds, and learning can now take place anywhere—with anyone. Where students used to have pen pals to learn from kids in far away places, now assignments can be given for students to work with collaborative partners—immediately.

Even teachers are taking advantage of the online collaborative sessions. Rather than traveling across the district to work with a group of colleagues, teachers can now work seamlessly with other teachers regardless of their current location. The only thing they need is access to the file through programs like Google Docs, Wikispaces, Dropbox, and more. What a great way to save time and effort—bring work to you instead of the other way around!

> I love collaborating with my students, parents, and other authentic audiences. It gives students a real purpose to produce quality work. (Karen Chichester, personal communication, January 12, 2014)

Beyond working together in the classroom, having students work in the Cloud allows them to collaborate with others from the "real world." Whether it's bringing in a guest lecturer through Google Hangouts or having a NASA scientist share a presentation with your kids, the Cloud gives students the chance to share and learn in practical learning environments.

Provide Immediate Feedback

One of the best ways to help students improve their work is by providing immediate feedback. Collaborating in the Cloud gives teachers real-time access to student projects and enables educators to make guided comments on students' work. Having this type of immediate response is a great asset to students because they can right their course early in a project. In a traditional writing project, teachers share feedback with the students after the final draft is submitted; now it can happen at any point in the process.

As Karen Chichester stated, "The Cloud has allowed me to support struggling learners whenever they need it and wherever they are. It has broken down the walls" (personal communication, January 5, 2014).

Over the next few chapters we delve into collaborating in the Cloud as we learn from classroom teachers how they are using programs like Google Docs, Edmodo, and Wikispaces. You'll see how you can get students working together on projects and find examples of teachers using the Cloud to collaborate with each other.

GOOGLE DOCS

Bird's Eye View: Five Things to Know About Google Docs

1. Google Docs allows students and teachers to edit documents in real time.

2. Users can expand Google Docs with a variety of Add-ons to increase the usefulness of a document.

3. Google Docs can be shared securely using e-mail addresses rather than attachments.

4. Teachers can work with students on writing projects using Editing, Suggesting, and Viewing modes.

5. Writing tools include Research, Translate, Define, and more.

What Is Google Docs?

Source: ©Google 2014

Google Docs has been around for years, but this amazing tool keeps getting better. Originally, Docs had very basic word processing tools that allowed users to create documents online. Now, this tool has become a "go to" for collaborative writing projects in the Cloud. Multiple students can work on the same file, and their contributions are seen in real time. It's also made life easier for teachers regarding grading because they can share suggestions and corrections in student projects quickly and efficiently.

Google Docs Features

You may feel like you already know Google Docs, but let's take a moment to look at some of the latest features. Recently, there have been some major new additions that will help you and your students get the most from this amazing tool.

Working on Documents

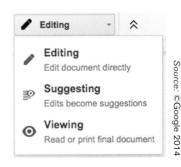

Writing projects may never be the same again. Google Docs makes it easier than ever to switch between writing and reviewing student work. With three different modes for working on documents—Editing, Suggesting, and Viewing— now individuals and groups can seamlessly work through a piece of writing.

Source: ©Google 2014

Editing. The best aspect of Google Docs is the ease in editing documents online. Teachers and students have access to all the major editing tools and any changes to a document are saved automatically. Students can also revert the document back to a previous version using the Revision History under the File menu. This means that your document is backed up along with all the edits that have been made for the history of the document.

Suggesting. A new tool in Google Docs enables editors to make suggestions in a document. Set up like Track Changes in Microsoft Word, suggestions inserts the suggestions into the document and allows the owner to accept or reject the edits. This provides teachers with the ability to make suggestions in student projects easily without mandating the changes. This is also a great way for students to work together in a peer review project.

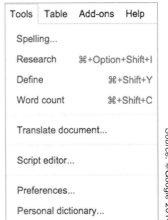

Source: ©Google 2014

Viewing. Once a document is complete, the owner can move the file into Viewing mode. This immediately removes all the editing controls and cleans the document up as it's ready for final draft stage. Students changing their documents into Viewing mode signals to the teacher that it's time to review the final work.

Awesome Editing Tools

Google Docs truly takes advantage of the online space and provides users easy access to tools that can improve their writing and benefit their audience. Found under the Tools menu, be sure to check out some of the following features:

Research. This is another hidden gem in Google Docs. Clicking on Research opens up a search window along the right side of your document. Here Google will provide you with basic search results for the topic it recognizes in your document. You can refine the search using a variety of filters that include Images, Videos, Scholar, Web, and more.

Define. Use the Define tool to open up an interactive dictionary along the right side of your document. You'll be able to define the word in a variety of built-in languages. This is a great tool to help your students pick the right word.

Translate. Click on the Translate Document option and you'll be able to translate your document into a variety of different languages. The best part is that Google will create a copy of your document in the new language, meaning you'll still maintain the original version.

Expanding Google Docs

For years people have complained that Google Docs couldn't keep up with Microsoft Word for the number of tools and different features that were part of the famous ribbon. Google, they claimed, was a watered-down version of the word processor and couldn't be used except for the simplest of writing projects. Well, those days are a thing of the past.

Recently Google released a new menu in the Google Doc interface: Add-ons. This tool allows users access to a repository of extensions created by third-party developers that extend the power of your Google Docs. By simply clicking on the Add-ons menu and choosing Get Add-ons, you can find any number of tools that will improve your document. The best part is that once a feature has been added to your version of Google Docs it remains for any future documents you create. Extensions are categorized in a variety of different fields, and the Education area contains a lot of useful tools for teachers and students. Here are a few Add-ons worth noting:

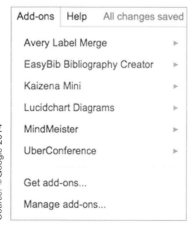

gMath. Math teachers rejoice! gMath allows users to type complex math formulas into their documents. Additionally, you can use the tool to chart and graph formulas that are easily added to your documents.

Kaizena. Kaizena allows teachers to create voice feedback as part of their assessments on student writing. By simply highlighting some text and launching the tool, educators can record their comments and embed them right into student projects. What a great way to personalize your feedback to students.

EasyBib. Add EasyBib to Google Docs and citing sources for your next research project will be a snap! EasyBib allows users to search an online tool to find the references for books, articles, and websites. Once found, the resources can be cited in MLA, APA, or Chicago Style. With a final click, the citation is added to your document and you're done. The research paper may never be the same again!

MindMeister. This Add-on creates amazing graphic organizers from your content. Just highlight the outline in your next writing project and MindMeister will turn your list into a mind map in one click. This is a great way to help your students visualize content.

Sharing Your Google Doc

Even though it's not a new feature, don't forget that one of the biggest changes in bringing documents to the Cloud is the ability to provide access. Access can mean having the ability to work on the document from a variety of locations on several different devices, but the access that matters most for teachers and students is being able to provide access to their work. Collaboration is a central component in the classroom of today, and Google Docs gives users the ability to work with others in an effective manner.

In the past, sharing a file with someone else required using e-mail or portable storage to facilitate the transfer. However, one big problem with sharing files this way is that copies of documents are created. Having multiple copies of a file is a management nightmare for many users.

Google Docs makes file sharing simple. Rather than sending the document to collaborators via e-mail, sharing means sharing access to the online document. This means there is only one document, not several versions of a shared file.

Once a document is shared, the power in Google Docs is clear; real-time editing where everyone involved can work with one another. Projects that once had lots of downtime while you waited your turn to make contributions now happen instantly. Sure, you'll need to ensure that collaborators don't type on top of one another, but Google Docs makes sharing easy.

Down in the Trenches

Let's take a closer look at how Nick Reilly from Edmonton has been implementing Google Drive with his classes.

I've been using Google Docs in my classroom for the last 4 years. My students and I have enjoyed using it to do many different projects, and we've always been open to suggestions on how to use it for something new. Many of my students have continued to use Google services even after they have left my classroom because it is a districtwide initiative, but are quick to share their current work when they want me to take a look at something, or give them feedback.

I've found students are actively engaged when working with technology to create things, and Google's services within Drive have given them latitude to create many different things. The two lessons that I'll be linking work from are vastly different in subject matter, but both came from student suggestion about "why can't we use Google for this?" Improvements were made along the way, and I intend on using both assignments in the future.

The first assignment is Language Arts based, where we started with narrative story writing. Many of my students were lamenting the way that their fairy tales had to end a certain way to fit into an archetype, and we decided that for our next writing project we would take a look at stories with different endings. Enter the "Choose Your Own Adventure" series of novels from the late 1980s to 1990s. We decided to map out our ideas for different endings and then work backward to our beginnings. Our finished product used hyperlinking in Google Docs to create a living document that "jumped to pages" based on which choice our readers made. Here are two examples (http://bit.ly/1GyURaf) and (http://bit.ly/1IFUIIH) that used our Summer Camp template. We worked as a group on a shared write, and I showed the kids how to make a bookmark and a link. The kids were engaged throughout the assignment, and many of them went back to work on their stories on their own time to add endings after we'd moved on to other things.

The second assignment is Science based, where we have an Evidence and Investigation unit. The unit requires us to talk about recognizing patterns, evidence of human disturbance, linking evidence to suspects by classification, and to understand how unique characteristics of evidence can allow investigators to make inferences. We do a bunch of experiments, and usually there is a crime scene that the kids get to participate in at the end of the unit as a culminating activity. I decided that rather than taking the kids through a crime scene, they could create their own. We created a top-down sketch of some houses together so that they understood the basics of what was needed to create their drawing first. Then we talked about what kinds of evidence would be found at a typical crime scene, and the kids brainstormed some answers. We then talked about how all this would be brought together. We decided that we'd need a list of the evidence found, along with a labeled diagram of where it was found in the scene. Then we added a list of suspects and how they were linked to the victim or the crime. Some of the kids had three or four

Source: Used with permission of Nick Reilly.

Nick Reilly

Teacher

Edmonton Public School Board

Edmonton, Alberta

Twitter: @NotebookNick

Recommended Tool to Explore: Lucidpress

documents, linked together for different floors or to their list. Here's an example of a list (http://bit.ly/1Tc4Be1) and a diagram (http://bit .ly/1MJtvgK) using Google Docs and Drawings. Looking back, there's much better software out there that's emerging to create floor plans linked to Google services. Floorplanner (http://bit.ly/1B3ciO5) was one that I used this year to create an "ideal learning space" and had students write about what their space needed. When looking at doing this assignment this year, I'll be taking another look at software that's available before assigning it.

A Student's View

From Coleton R., Grade 11:

Google Docs allows me to do group projects easily in school. It also knows when I am typing in another language and spell-checks in the other language which makes it convenient for me to use. Google Docs is something I use everyday and any student can benefit from using it!

Why Use Google Docs?

Google Docs has changed the way many think about creating and sharing documents. Before it was all about the software you had on your computer, and now the only thing that matters is having an Internet connection. Google Docs is the ultimate collaboration tool for teachers and students. It makes sharing your files easy and safe, while providing users the tools they need to expand their projects in a multitude of ways. Google Docs is the granddaddy of Cloud tools for a reason—it's the one tool no classroom can do without!

Taking It to a Higher Level

• Use comments to share ideas on an article. Engage your students in a close reading of a document or PDF you upload into Google Docs. You can have your students share their thoughts on key points in the article. Also, students can comment to one another in addition to sharing original ideas.

• Explore revision history to evaluate student contributions. One of the biggest challenges when students work in a group is determining each student's contributions. Try using Revision History to look at each and every character from all members of the group. Because Google Docs saves after every change in a document, this is an easy way to determine overall contributions from every student.

• Google Docs now has the ability to edit Microsoft Word files without converting them. One of the challenges of converting files from Microsoft's style to that of Google Docs is that some of your formatting can be altered. Images may get displaced in the document or tables can have issues. Now Google Docs allows edits of Microsoft Word files, without converting them into a Google Doc.

EDMODO

Bird's Eye View: Five Things to Know About Edmodo

1. No subscriptions, extra software, or extra hardware purchase necessary.
2. Edmodo offers collaboration in a secure, closed environment.
3. Students have 24/7 access to their documents in their Cloud-based "Backpack."
4. A built-in survey tool allows teachers to check comprehension.
5. Embeddable objects (Prezi, YouTube videos, Google Forms, etc.) can be shared.

What Is Edmodo?

Source: ©Edmodo 2014

The most common way that Edmodo is described is the "Facebook" for education. That is a good description, but it does not tell the full story. Edmodo is a social media platform that allows students and teachers to connect in a private and secure environment outside the classroom. It allows the learning to extend beyond the regular school hours and creates a space for teachers to share all the resources that can enhance the classroom experience.

Edmodo was created by teachers to provide a deeper connection with students after the final bell rings for the day. Teachers can place many different types of resources (videos, handouts, links, etc.) for students to explore on their own at home. There is a built-in comment section that allows conversation to take place on the items shared by teachers and discussions that took place earlier in the day. Edmodo is the digital space that can become the perfect extension to the classroom.

One of the great things about Edmodo is that it can become what teachers need it to for their specific class. It can become an extension of class discussion by allowing students to post comments and respond to their peers. It can be the place that allows teachers to collect work and return to students for review. It can be a single stop for students to find valuable resources shared by the teacher to further their understanding of a lesson. Teachers can create groups and see what all the students are working on in the group discussion. With this flexibility, Edmodo can be the right tool for every teacher no matter how they want to use it.

Edmodo Features

Edmodo on the Fly

Edmodo has amazing apps on iTunes and Google Play Store that students and teachers can use to access their accounts and continue their work on the go. More and more students are using their mobile devices as their prime computing device and they will need to access class content on their device. Edmodo has a wonderful mobile app that allows students access to their work whenever they want, wherever they are.

Edmodo has a smooth interface and allows students and teachers the same access to information they would have on their desktop computer. Teachers will have access to their grade book and can be notified when students leave comments on their posts. Students can access the documents shared by teachers and engage in the conversation taking place on topics shared by the teacher and other students. Edmodo will send push notifications to the mobile device as well, so teachers and students can be alerted immediately when there has been an update.

There's an App for That

Edmodo also has a great collection of apps that can allow the teacher to personalize their Edmodo space they create for their students. There are free apps and paid apps that can enhance the Edmodo experience in different ways. EduClipper is available for free and can allow students and teachers the ability to curate content and access it on Edmodo. There is also a Frog Dissection paid app that can allow students to practice at home before class dissection or possibly use it as an alternative to a real frog in class. The app directory is growing every day and can really help teachers create the best experience for their students.

Down in the Trenches

Jennifer Bond is a third-grade teacher and an Edmodo Certified Trainer. She has many great uses of Edmodo to share. Let's hear her story:

Edmodo, a social learning network for the classroom, has been one of the most impactful Cloud tools I have used with my third graders over the years. I consider it to be the digital hub of my classroom, our go-to place on the Internet. From adding videos that support learning to embedding maps and having my students identify natural and human features, I found many uses for Edmodo. I have also found it to be a great tool to connect with other educators, and it has increased my Professional Learning Network by leaps and bounds.

Working with third graders, I have found Edmodo to be very helpful to organize the tasks for my students during our BYOD Days, as well as our computer lab time. I often create a post with our tasks that include the directions, as well as the links to the sites they need to go to. In addition, I am able to utilize the apps for Edmodo, both free and paid, for the students to use. The benefit of using the apps in Edmodo is it eliminates the students having to remember an extra username and password, as well as the time it takes to register a class. Many of the apps within Edmodo are the same apps that classrooms are already using, like Spelling City, Moby Max, and Go Animate to name a few.

In my classroom, I have BYOD Days twice a week. On these days, I try to incorporate technology choices for assignments throughout the day. Due to the diversity of the devices, a tool that crosses all platforms is essential. Edmodo is the perfect tool, and it is the main way students complete and turn in assignments. Students have the ability to take photos with their devices and add them directly to their Edmodo Backpack, which is their Cloud-based folder. From screenshots of Minecraft creations to Geometric Photo Hunts, students are able to present their learning easily. Since I don't have dongles for each device, pulling up the posts in Edmodo on my laptop is just as easy when we are closing lessons.

After learning about nonfiction text features, students went on a nonfiction text feature hunt. Searching for the features in real books from our classroom library, textbooks in their desks, or eBooks, students were able to take screenshots or photos and add them to their backpack in Edmodo. The end result was great because students had a wide range of features they found during the hunt and were able to share them with their classmates. In addition, the work they completed will always be in their backpack to use in the future.

(Continued)

(Continued)

The posts that my students complete can often have mechanical errors. The great thing about Edmodo is that the teacher can have all editing rights to every post within the group, which allows me to pull up posts and edit them as a class. This provides students with an authentic experience, and I have noticed that students in turn begin to peer edit on their own by commenting to posts.

My class participated in the Holiday Card Exchange, a great way to connect with classrooms all over the United States and Canada sponsored by Projects by Jen (www.projectsbyjen.com). Each student was assigned a school to create a card for, and I wanted them to get to know where their card was being sent. In the computer lab, students looked up the school's address using Google Maps and then used the embed code to post it to our Edmodo group. They then wrote what they noticed around the area of the school such as landforms, geographical references, businesses, homes, and so on. Students were so excited to discover new things about their world and make connections to the classrooms that would be receiving their holiday card.

Speaking of collaborative projects, Edmodo is home to one of the biggest collaborative projects, The Global Read Aloud (http://theglobalreadaloud.com). Each year hundreds of teachers and classrooms connect to share their experiences with great books. It is great because teachers join one large organizational group, but then eventually use the power of connection to form smaller groups. Students are able to connect on Edmodo with other classrooms from around the globe to share ideas, projects, and build literary partnerships that can extend into other parts of the curriculum.

Here's a tip that I learned from Liz Keheler, the Learning Programs Manager at Edmodo, and a tip that has modified the way I use Edmodo. One of the features Edmodo offers to teachers is the ability to create small groups. I have several small groups for my classroom. I have book club groups for kids, math enrichment groups, project planning groups, team groups for Destination Imagination, and so on. These groups usually only have seven or less kids in them. When working with Liz, she showed me that you can leverage small groups to organize your group better. There is an option to move all your students in the group to the small group. What this does is make a sub group for all the posts and assignments. I have used this for special projects that I knew we were going to work on for a couple of weeks. For example, our Valentine's Day cards were all posted in a small group. This saved me time, because I did not have to scroll through the entire main feed from a 2-week period to search for posted digital Valentine's Day cards. Using small groups in Edmodo can be a timesaver and a great organization tool! Give it a try!

What makes a great digital tool better? Students who think that it is a great tool! My third graders love Edmodo. They feel like they have their own group to hang with outside of school, just like their own Facebook. I asked one of my students to write her feelings about Edmodo, and I would like to share it with you.

Source: Used with permission of Jennifer Bond.

Jennifer Bond

Third-Grade Teacher

Walled Lake, Michigan

Twitter: @TeamBond

Website: edtechcheerleader.com

A Student's View

How Edmodo Has Impacted My Learning

By Maddie T.

I have used Edmodo in many different ways. From sharing many moments to doing an assignment, Edmodo has it all. One thing I have used Edmodo for is creating short stories and posting them to the class. I also love connecting with the class after school and sharing ideas and many different thoughts. I have also posted several websites and videos to the class to help them learn more about the world around them. Our teacher, Mrs. Bond, has posted lots of different assignments for the class to do such as math problems, nonfiction writing, story problems, and so much more! It is almost like homework; however, it is more fun, and it's digital! Another reason I like Edmodo is that Mrs. Bond created a small group (on Edmodo) for me

(Continued)

(Continued)

and some other classmates to create a homepage for a little business we have called T Spa. We post new programs, sugar scrubs, and sales on there! I have also used the backpack on Edmodo to put photos in and share them with the class! Although there are many, many different and interesting things about Edmodo, the thing I like best is being with my class and teacher always. So thank you, Mrs. Bond, for connecting me with Edmodo, and thank you, Edmodo, for connecting me with the world.

Why Use Edmodo?

For teachers, Edmodo makes sense as a perfect way to extend the classroom to allow for conversations to continue after the period ends. It allows teachers to consolidate all their resources into one location that can be updated from their mobile device with the Edmodo app. Grading and feedback are a breeze for teachers and helps create a paperless environment. Edmodo is a great option for teachers looking to create a safe online environment for students to continue their learning outside the classroom.

For students, Edmodo allows them access to all their assignments the teacher has posted, as well as a collection of resources to aid in understanding. The mobile apps allow the student to access all the same information when they are away from their desktop. Students can also continue the class conversation after the final bell to grow their understanding of a topic covered in class. Group projects and staying connected in class have never been easier for students in the classroom.

Taking It to a Higher Level

- By using the Groups feature, a teacher could create a Literature Circle so student can discuss independent reading online and extend class discussions.

- Parents can create accounts and join classes to keep track of the work assigned in class.

- Edmodo allows teachers to connect with other teachers and classrooms. This can allow classes from all over the world to work together on amazing projects.

WIKISPACES

Bird's Eye View: Five Things to Know About Wikispaces

1. A wiki is a great collaborative space where students can share ideas and work in online groups.
2. Wikispaces Classroom is designed to provide teachers with lots of interactive and assessment tools.
3. Projects give the teacher the ability to design assignments for differentiated instruction.
4. Users can upload or embed a variety of multimedia file types in a wiki.
5. Wikispaces provides a closed online environment, providing a secure space for students to work and communicate with one another.

What Is Wikispaces?

Wikispaces has taken the traditional website and transformed it into a collaborative workspace. Where the web used to be a one-way communication device, with the teacher sharing information with students and parents, now Wikispaces provides access for different groups to work with one another. It is a great way to for both students and teachers to share in the classroom learning!

Source: @Wikispaces 2014

Wikispaces Features

Wikispaces Classroom allows you to create your classroom online. Teachers using Wikispaces Classroom can develop the same types of activities that are successful in their classrooms including discussions, assignments, assessments, and more.

Teachers can use Wikispaces Classroom to set up announcements and message boards for students. Having a social media component in a safe, closed environment is a great way to permit students to talk with one another about assignments and more. Students will love the access to a "social network" and parents will like the safety controls that keep kids in a monitored online space. This is a great way for the teacher to share his or her message with both parents and students, while also instructing the class on appropriate ways to communicate online.

One of the best features of Wikispaces Classroom is the ability to create assignments for specific groups of learners. The teacher has complete control over how to release assignments, and he or she can use various assignments to help differentiate the learning for the classroom.

Another new feature of Wikispaces Classroom is real-time assessment. Teachers can monitor student progress in real time as kids are working on assignment in the class wiki. This is a great way to track each student's progress and allows the teacher time to intervene with kids who are falling behind.

Enhance Learning With Media

Wikispaces is a terrific space for incorporating a variety of multimedia learning objects into any online lesson. Teachers can easily embed video clips or images that benefit visual learners. Google Forms and other survey tools allow educators quick insights into student understanding.

Students can work collaboratively using various tools included in the class wiki. Instead of simply accessing text on the web, students can share lots of different widgets as part of their learning.

Down in the Trenches

Blair Einfeldt teaches Language Arts in the Sweetwater School District #1 in Rock Springs, WY. He has incorporated Wikispaces into several different writing activities in his classroom. Let's explore his story:

I am a backwards thinker so to speak. I like to think of my journey as a teacher in terms of destination first, vehicle type second, and then specific make and model third. As an English teacher, I knew there were things the state wanted me to teach, that common core was going to be another stop along the way (metaphorically and actual), and I knew I had my own standards. With that being said, two years ago, I mapped out the destination to which I wanted to take my students. It looked similar to this:

I wanted my students to

- find a more authentic audience than just me as a teacher and their peers,
- be able to work collaboratively within their class,
- be able to work collaboratively outside the walls of their class,
- utilize meaningful technology (21st century skills) to create something they are proud of and can show off, and
- have access to their work from anywhere in the world.

I had received a full iPad lab for my class that school year and knew that I would have Internet and word-processing resources literally at my students' fingertips. I began looking for different programs that provided the above-mentioned criteria. I came across Wikispaces from a suggestion from a fellow teacher. They used Wikispaces as a class-room website; however, I wanted to use it a bit differently. I wanted to use it as almost a group, collaborative portfolio.

We tried it out with a lit circle. In this situation, I took all four of my classes and basically created lit circles for different novels we were reading. Wikispaces allowed me to divide my students into teams, one for each book. Instead of having your typical in-class groups, this time I was able to create a collaborative workspace for students to work together without the barriers of classroom walls. Each group was in charge of basically creating a wiki for their book. They divided up jobs and had pages for characters, theme, plot, setting, analysis, and even had a discussion forum where they could talk about questions they had in the book. It allowed them basically an online, Cloud-based, reference spot for everything they were learning in their books. This way, when it came time to present their novel and show an in-depth analysis, they were able to quickly reference images, characters, and information that they had generated as they went.

Wikispaces also provides an assessment tool where I was able to check both student involvement and engagement. It also allowed me to create mini incentives for people working on the wiki, and I had competitions to see who and/or what team could spend the most time working on the wiki, who had the most page edits, and who had the most activity of the discussion threads.

Check out our Wikispaces page at http://readerschoice14.wiki spaces.com.

(Continued)

(Continued)

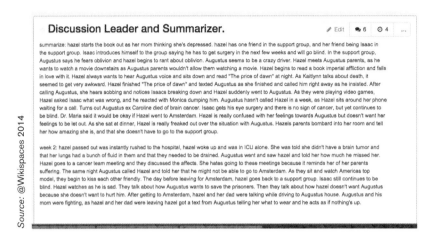

Source: @Wikispaces 2014

Example of a discussion forum that I generated at the beginning of the unit. The rest were all student-generated questions. (I gave some examples of open-ended questions to discuss.)

Source: @Wikispaces 2014

Example of a team page created by one group on the book they read. This page included a brief synopsis, a link to a group-made trailer (one part of the assignment) on YouTube, and links to each of the individual pages (e.g., characters, analysis, thematic elements, vocabulary words, cultural connections, aphorisms or important quotes).

This is how the unit was structured:

3-week unit

3-day cycles (1 day pointed deep reading instruction, 1 day reading day, 1 day wiki work, then repeat)

Each member of the group was in charge of a job for the week. They had until Sunday night to complete their job. If the job was not completed on Wikispaces by Sunday, their job went into a classified section in their group for extra work and their group members could steal the points for the job and do the work. This created a much higher premium for on-time work.

At the end, the students presented their books in a video format using screenshots and information from Wikispaces. The videos were placed on the front page of their Wikispaces team page.

Wikispaces completely incorporated everything I was looking for and more. The students loved it because they could do their work at home, at school, or even on their phones or tablets. We also had a social media competition to see which team could get the most likes on Facebook with the social media share option. It really created an opportunity for the students to be not only proud of their work, but also provided a more real-world audience. The students' work was much higher because they had to do something that was not just acceptable to the teacher, but acceptable to their friends. It is funny how much more pressure the students feel to look good in front of the Internet, as opposed to their teacher. Wikispaces naturally provides that level of accountability.

It was also nice to not need another app and that this could be accessed through any web browser on any device.

One of my favorite parts of Wikispaces was the message option. Students who were having problems on the wiki were able to message me outside of class, and I could respond to them in real time if need be. I love the ability as a teacher to have, what I call, God-like power over the wiki. If any discussions get into the realm of unnecessary, I can delete them. If anything is plagiarized, I can easily check that. If any student is struggling with any part of their page, I can access it and give them quick help AT ANY TIME.

Last, from a teacher's standpoint, Wikispaces provides you with a real tangible example of many of the things that administrators are looking for. In my case, my administrator doesn't know my content area, so when he looks at my class, he is looking for a few things:

1. Student engagement

2. Clear expectations and communication with students

(Continued)

(Continued)

3. Common Core alignment

4. Transparency

5. Teaching and demonstrating 21st century skills

Wikispaces provides all these in a bundled package.

1. Students are engaged, and you can view and monitor engagement. Most important, it provides a printout of their engagement, which can help document that aspect.

2. I was able to put each rubric, each requirement in clear language on the main wiki page. That way, students have little to no excuse of not understanding the expectations.

3. I aligned my assignments with Common Core and was able to post links to which specific Core Standard it dealt with. My administrator ATE THAT UP!

4. The transparency of having all your work readily available anywhere creates trust with building administrators.

5. It is obvious that students will be demonstrating 21st century skills through remote collaborative work, digital portfolios, and alignment across multiple digital devices.

I was interviewed by Wikispaces in conjunction with this assignment. The interview can be found at https://www.youtube.com/watch?v=wJpmM897KYY.

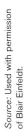

Source: Used with permission of Blair Einfeldt.

Blair Einfeldt

Eleventh- and Twelfth-Grade Language Arts Teacher

Rock Springs High School

Rock Springs, WY

Twitter: @blaireinfeldt

Website/blog: https://sites.google.com/site/rshsnerdycoach/

Recommended Tools to Explore: I love all things Google, but Aurasma is a fun tool to use instead of presentations. Our end wiki presentation was done via Aurasma and digitally attached to the cover of their book like a QR code on steroids.

A Student's View

From Hannah C., Grade 10:

Wikispaces combines all the things that make education through technology so great. It has nearly every single unique feature that other platforms offer in isolation.

Why Use Wikispaces?

Wikispaces provides teachers with an open collaborative workplace to work with students. Rather than a static website that only gives publishing access to the instructor, a wiki allows everyone in class to make contributions to the learning environment. Wikispaces Classroom really moves this platform to the next level and provides teachers with a variety of options for designing and assessing student work. Classroom's use of the social media platform is something that students love and parents feel comfortable with as part of closed classroom environment.

Taking It to a Higher Level

- Create a classroom encyclopedia. Have students create their own entries in a shared classroom encyclopedia. Students can each research a topic and write an article to be shared in the class wiki. The kids can use images, video, polls, and more to bring the topic to life.

- Student webpages: A wiki is a great way to have your students create an online portfolio of their work. They can use the wiki to share assignments and reflect on their learning. Beyond working individually, you can also have students create a webpage in small groups as a different way to collect and present content.

- Build your class resource page. Rather than having students search the web to find great content, you can build a link list to share a "student-friendly" website with your students. Even better, if students have the rights to contribute to the wiki, they can add sites they find to the list.

4

Creating in the Cloud

Creating in the Cloud is something that has become much more prevalent in classrooms, and it has created many questions along the way. Some people believe that there are ownership issues when it comes to creating in the Cloud and others who do not believe that is a legitimate concern and embrace the wonderful things that can be done in the Cloud. Creating in the Cloud offers students and educators so many more possibilities than the traditional format of creating. Lessons no longer have to be confined to a single notebook, and projects can be completed from anywhere in the world. Collaboration has been taken to new heights with Cloud-based creation, and students could not be happier. Some educators might be a bit hesitant to create in the Cloud, but there are many great opportunities to amazing things when students and teachers create in the Cloud.

There have been many concerns expressed about the ownership of content created using Cloud-based tools. Google came under fire when they released Google Drive because many people feared that Google would own all their work and urban legends circulated that Google was publishing books others had created and keeping the royalties. These are not true. As a matter of fact, Google explicitly states that users retain all ownership rights to their materials. Skydrive from Microsoft and Dropbox have also put users at ease by clearly stating that users own their content. These fears come from users not completely trusting others with their personal documents. Cloud-based companies have done a much better job educating people on how their data is saved. Still, there are fears regarding the safety of their created content in the Cloud that is worth exploring.

There are many people who are afraid to create content in the Cloud because of the fear it might not be there in the morning. These are legitimate fears. There is an aspect of trust that users must have when it comes to storing their work in a Cloud-based network. It is important for users to do research on the site they want to use to keep their created content. If it is a large company like Google or Prezi, there should be a high level of trust because of the number of users they have. If it is a smaller startup trying to find a space to grow, there is a risk the company could fold and the data created and saved on this site could be lost. Like any tool, it is important for users to do research to see if it fits all their needs. There will always be some risk of creating in the Cloud, but the benefits outweigh the risks. Kyle Pace said it best: "We're doing students a disservice if we don't allow them to connect, collaborate, and create in all the great online spaces the Cloud offers us."

Creating in the Cloud offers all users the opportunity to create a more dynamic workflow. In the past, users would create on their own computer and would be stuck with a tough decision when it came to sharing that content. They could use a floppy disk or flash drive to transfer the file from one computer to the other, but there were potential problems creators could face. If the computer the content was going to be opened on next did not have the correct program, the content was useless. Also, if anything happened to the disk or drive, the content would be lost. If the user-created content was too large, e-mail would not be an option and the content would be stuck on the computer. Cloud-based creation helped solve all these problems. Prezi is a great example of this. A user can create a Prezi and access this presentation anywhere there is an Internet connection. The Prezi can be opened on a phone and edited and then saved for later use on a desktop computer. Large content can be created and accessed by opening a new browser window and accessing the site. Lost flash drives are a worry of the past. Content can be created and viewed at any time from any location regardless of the programs available on the device. This allows great flexibility when it comes to creating in the Cloud. Collaboration also changes workflow when content is created in the Cloud.

Groupwork used to be the bane of many students' existence before Cloud-based technology became a regular part of creating. Trying to coordinate the different schedules of everyone in the group so they could all work on the same document was a very difficult task. If it was not possible, the frustration of creating a document and e-mailing it around could be seen across all their faces as they presented the incorrect version to the teacher in class. Cloud-based tools have changed the collaboration game and the workflow of users around the world. Students now have the freedom to work on projects at times that are best for them. It is great if the entire group can be together and work face-to-face, but that is not always an option. Using Cloud-based tools to create and collaborate allows students to work from the comfort of their home, a local coffee shop, or grandma's house on the weekend. Student Kathryn P. had this to say about working in the Cloud:

> Before Cloud-based tech became mainstream, my group members and I would have to set a time and a place to meet the old-fashioned way. It was always inconvenient for at least one person to meet up (they live across campus or it's too late at night for them to go out, etc.). Now that I'm a senior and Cloud-based technology is more widespread, using video chatting technologies, such as Skype or FaceTime makes it so much easier to "meet up" with everyone, since the group can work from wherever is convenient for each individual, while discussing the project as though everyone is together.

Students are living in a world where connecting needs to be quick and easy. . . .

Educators can benefit from creating in the Cloud as well.

The standard lesson plan book is something teachers have held sacred for many years. These books held all the important information for the coming year, and losing it would be disastrous for any teacher. Today, keeping all this important information in one place seems crazy. Cloud-based tools allow teachers to create their content and have it available whenever they want and wherever they are. By creating these lessons in the Cloud, the teacher has more access to their own information. That is so important for teachers. Too often new ideas come to a teacher's mind, but they are lost on scraps of paper before they can be saved someplace safe. Teachers' workflow no longer has to revolve around their desk or desktop computer. By creating in the Cloud, teachers will be able to edit content when they have time and wherever they feel comfortable. If a teacher's workflow can be streamlined, that opens up more time for students in the classroom and family time at home. Besides a streamlined workflow for users, greater access is another great reason to create in the Cloud.

A common concern many teachers have when it comes to using technology in the classroom is access. It is important to make sure that students have access to the different programs that teachers are using in the classroom. Creating in the Cloud can help alleviate these concerns. Kyle Calderwood addresses this concern, "The greatest benefit is that it is device agnostic. No more worrying about who is on what platform!" Kyle makes an excellent point. Cloud-based tools allow users to access the same information regardless of the device they are using. Many of the most popular Cloud-based tools—Google Apps, Prezi, Evernote, and others—have mobile apps. These apps allow users to access the content no matter what type of device they have. Barriers to learning can be tough for students to over-come on their own, so it is important for teachers to make sure that content is as accessible as possible. While some students might not have access to a traditional computer at home, it is more likely that they have access to a computer in their pocket. Since many Cloud-based tools do not require a specific operating system, students can work on the device that is best for them. The same can be said for teachers as well.

Having a Mac at home and working in a PC district is no longer an issue for teachers. By creating in the Cloud, a teacher can access all their work from any computer with a working Internet connec-tion. This is also wonderful for the teachers in the classroom because they will no longer have to worry about compatibility issues with stu-dent work. By modeling Cloud-based creation for students, teachers no longer have to worry about the students not being able to display their work in class because they used a different platform to create. This allows the teacher to give students more options when it comes to creating for class. By giving students more options, it also allows the teachers to expand their lesson plans. The teacher does not have to worry about programs for specific computers when the assignment utilizes Cloud-based programs. As teachers further explore the dif-ferent options with Cloud-based creations, lessons can become more engaging for the students who can access them from the device of their choosing.

Creating in the Cloud is something that is powerful, but it does raise some questions of ownership. With a little research, users will see that Cloud-based technology ensures that users own their work and all their ideas even when they create using their product. By using Cloud-based creation tools, teachers and students can streamline their workflow, collaborate more freely, and no longer worry about com-patibility issues. Access is crucial as educators look to reach students and engage them in the classroom. Allowing students to use Cloud-based tools opens up a new world of creation to them.

INSTAGRAM

Bird's Eye View: Five Things to Know About Instagram

1. Instagram allows users to tag photos to quickly sort images into categories. This can be content related or based on a specific activity.

2. Instagram works on mobile devices that have a digital camera and are Internet ready.

3. Photos can be edited in many different ways using filters that encourage student creativity.

4. Hashtags allows users to search for public photos based on keywords.

5. Instagram doesn't allow photo uploads in a browser.

What Is Instagram?

One of the most popular uses of mobile devices is the digital camera. Students love taking pictures of the world around them. Instagram allows students to share these photos with a larger audience, including parents, peers, and more. By sharing their photos beyond the classroom walls, students can extend their learning.

Source: @Instagram 2014

Instagram Features

Instagram uses a variety of filters to give users freedom to be creative with their photos. One of the big options for many Instagramers is the ability to make their photos look unique with filters that can easily be applied. Students love using the filters because they can make images appear as photos from previous decades. Even though the editing tools are basic in nature, they are still effective and allow students to let their creative juices flow.

How Does It Work?

Instagram is a free service that is straightforward to use and easy to adapt to a classroom setting. Users take photos using the camera in their tablet or cell phone and upload them to Instagram using the mobile app. The app is free and easy to set up for use. Images can be filtered by using hashtags, thus providing photo subjects a quick and easy way to be organized.

Finding Photos

Instagram users apply hashtags to their images to make them searchable. This means your students can find thousands of images related to various keywords. You can use these images to spark a conversation or guide a project based on a visual concept. Take a look at the #firstdayofschool and imagine having your students share thoughts about some of the different images and their implied meanings.

Down in the Trenches

Instagram is still relatively new in the classroom, but its impact is impressive. Lee Ann Lynds is a first-grade teacher from Alberta, Canada, who has used Instagram with her young students. Here is her story:

> I was trained in the Little Green Thumbs program in the fall of 2013. I wanted to share the experiences and changes of our classroom garden with the parents and students in the division. George Couros, the Division Principal of Innovative Teaching and Leaning for the Parkland School Division 70, suggested that I try Instagram. I used Instagram with my Grade 1 class so we would have a visual story line of our journey from seed to harvest. The students enjoyed checking the garden every day and sharing the changes observed in our garden on our Instagram account. We started our journey off by sharing the Instagram account with our parents (Instagram.com/pvsgreenthumbs). I found it an excellent tool to enhance the learning by making it a hands-on experience including many of the specific outcomes in the Grade One curriculum in Science, Math, Language Arts, and Health.
>
> In Science, we focused on Topic D: Senses and Topic E: Needs of Animals and Plants. (Senses 1–9: Students will use the senses to make general and specific observations and communicate observations orally and by producing captioned pictures.) We used our Five Senses to share changes in the garden over the entire process.

For example, the sense of smell helped us smell the spicy oregano; the sense of taste was used to describe the tastes when we tried unfamiliar or new plants such as dandelion tea, beans and other vegetables; the sense of sight was used to observe the daily changes;

Sight: The bean plant in the a.m.   The changes in the same plant in the p.m.

Source: ©Lee Ann Lynds 2014

Taste: Dandelion tea made from the leaves of dandelions.

Source: ©Lee Ann Lynds 2014

Our purple beans turned green and were sour.

(Continued)

(Continued)

the sense of touch was used to feel the vegetables, spices, dirt and seeds; and the sense of hearing was used to hear the ideas of our classmates and the humming sound of the electrical equipment used to keep the timers, light, and fans running.

(Needs of Plants 1–11: Students will describe common living things and identify needs of those living things.) Through our daily observations, attention was focused on how living things survive, what they need and how their needs are met. The students learned about their own responsibility in caring for living things. They identified the requirements of plants to maintain life, which are air, light, suitable temperature, water, growing medium, and space. They learned that we must provide these for the plants in our care in our garden for the plants to survive.

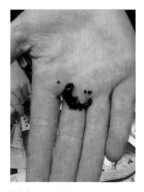

Source: ©Lee Ann Lynds 2014

Needs: Our light is on for 12 hours and off for 12 hours.

We learned about composting.

In addition to the primary core focus on Science we were able to tie in many other curriculum areas as part of our project.

In Math, we focused on Measurement. (Specific Outcome 1: Students will demonstrate an understanding of measurement as a process of comparing by identifying attributes that can be compared such as length/height, mass/weight, ordering objects by length/height, weight/mass, making statements of comparison by determining which of two or more given objects is the longest/shortest or heaviest/lightest by matching or comparing and explain the reasoning.) The students worked on determining which of the beans were the longest and how long it took the vegetables to grow to their maturity. We arranged our beans from the longest to the shortest. I challenged the children with questions such as, "How tall did the plants get?" "How much space did each plant need?"

Source: ©Lee Ann Lynds 2014

Tomato plant at 8 weeks old.   The same tomato plant at 11 weeks old.

Source: ©Lee Ann Lynds 2014

This is the same tomato plant at 17   Our longest bean was 17 cm long.
weeks. It is now 54 cm tall.

   In Health, we focused on healthy eating choices. (Wellness Choices
1.5: Students will recognize the importance of basic, healthy, nutri-
tional choices to well-being of self.) We discussed the importance of
the Canadian Food Guide and the amount of fruits and vegetables we
should consume daily for a healthy lifestyle. I found that the students
were willing to try different vegetables, fruits, and spices because they
had a part in growing the food.

(Continued)

(Continued)

In Language Arts, we focused on reading and writing: (a) General outcome 3.1 Plan and Focus—Focus attention and explore and share own ideas on topics of discussion and study. Determine information needs by asking and answering questions to satisfy information needs on a specific topic. Plan to gather information by following spoken directions for gathering ideas and information; (b) General outcome 3.3 Organize, Record and Evaluate—Organize information to identify categorize information according to sequence, or similarities and differences. List related ideas and information on a topic and make statements to accompany pictures. Record information to represent and explain key facts and ideas in own words. Evaluate information by recognizing and using gathered information to communicate new

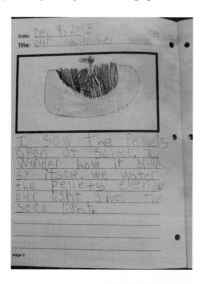 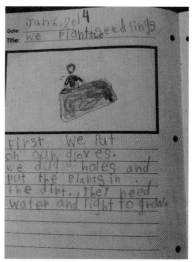

learning. We read the comments from the followers and practiced our writing by sharing our ideas on the Instagram account. We also kept a journal of the changes in our Little Green Thumbs Student Journals.

Part of the vision of Inspiring Education is for the Alberta Education system to support each student to become an engaged thinker "who uses technology to learn, innovate, communicate, and discover." According to Inspiring Education, technology "should play a broader role in the classroom. In addition to being used as a tool to impart information, ultimately its power should be harnessed in support of learners' innovation and discovery. It should be seamlessly integrated into the learning environment."

Instagram is an excellent tool to showcase the learning in an innovative learning environment where students take responsibility for their own learning and ideas. It is easy to set up and for Grade One and is a tool that can be used in so many curriculum areas to make learning hands-on and memorable. I am looking forward to using it with other projects in the future during my career as a teacher and educator.

Source: Used with permission of Lee-Ann Lynds.

Lee-Ann Lynds

Grade One Teacher

Parkland Village School

Alberta, Canada

Twitter: @pvsgreenthumbs and @LeeaLynds

Website/blog:
http://www.psdblogs.ca/llynds

A Student's View

Mason M., a student from our Grade One class, shares his insight on how Instagram impacted his learning in the classroom:

My parents allowed me to open my own Instagram account so that I could follow our Little Green Thumb project in my Grade One class. I got to observe the plants grow over time, and I was able to comment on the pictures that we posted on Instagram. It was fun to dig in the dirt and plant our seeds. My friends and my mom and dad left comments on my pictures and ideas that I shared. I would suggest that other teachers use Instagram as part of their learning because it is a fun way to learn.

Why Use Instagram?

Instagram is a wonderful tool for encouraging student creativity. Using Instagram allows teachers and students the opportunity to share their photos with a larger audience and helps build a sense of community with parents. It is easy to use and quick to share. Photos from class can be up and shared with others in a few clicks. This tool has revolutionized online photo sharing—it is an essential app for Cloud!

Taking It to a Higher Level

- Spotlight your students with a Student of the Day. This is a great way to highlight your amazing kids and share their accomplishments with a larger community.

- Have students recreate a famous piece of art or a moment from history. Visual learners will love the challenge of developing the setting for an historical recreation. Provide the kids with a copy of the original image, a few props, and let their imaginations soar!

- Turn your students into photojournalists. Have your students document a school or community event. Use #hashtags to share their images with different groups.

YOGILE

Bird's Eye View: Five Things to Know About Yogile

1. Yogile is a freemium service, meaning users can create a free account and add premium service features if desired.

2. Yogile allows photos to be shared to a single online album using an e-mail address.

3. Teachers can make the albums public or private using passwords.

4. Teachers can moderate photos from students, keeping inappropriate photos out of the album.

5. Photos are deleted from online albums after 14 days in basic accounts.

What Is Yogile?

Digital images are a great way for students to share what they've learned about a concept. One issue that plagues many teachers is how to quickly gather and display student images. Sure there are photo storage sites like Flickr; there are photo sharing sites like Facebook. But what are the options when you want to have a class of students share photos without having to become "friends" or forcing everyone to create another account for an online service?

Source: @Yogile 2014

Yogile is a freemium photo storage solution that allows teachers to create online photo albums to which students can easily share their digital photos.

Yogile Features

- **One Click to Start.** Getting started is easy; you can create an album with one click. Once you've created your online photo album, your students can start adding their images to the gallery.

+ Add Photo Album

Source: @Yogile 2014

- **Customized URL.** Once the album is created Yogile will provide you with a customized URL and e-mail. The e-mail is the key element, because you will have your students mail their photos to the online album straight from their mobile device.

- **Password Protect.** One of the benefits of Yogile is the ability to password protect your students' photos. Adding a password is simple, and it keeps your albums private to those outside your classroom community.

Down in the Trenches

Let's check in with Clint Stephens, an education technology specialist from the Southwestern Education Service Center in Cedar City, UT. Clint shares his practical experience from sharing digital images in his own classroom.

Many times in the classroom, photos taken by the teacher or by students are used for many reasons: to document group or project work, to show evidence of learning, to identify real-world examples, and so on. However, collecting, displaying and redistributing all these photos by the teacher back with the class can be a cumbersome process.

In the old-school days, I would have students bring digital cameras from home or use school cameras to go out and take photographs for certain lessons or activities. Then, I would gather all the cameras, do my best to connect them to my computer to import the photos, and then use a tool like Photoshop or iPhoto to export the photos to create a web page that I could post to my site so that the students could see all the photos taken for the activity or project. I found this activity to be very beneficial with my science students, but many teachers would not take the time nor would they have the knowledge and expertise to do this, especially in a timely manner.

Yogile.com has helped me streamline this process. Instead of gathering photos myself, I just need to set up an account and create a new album on Yogile. The service has a very clean layout and is very easy to use and discover what it can do. Once you have an album, Yogile will then:

- allow me to upload photos from my computer directly to the album;

- give me a custom e-mail address that **anyone** can use to post photos to the album by simply attaching them to the message—very easy to send from a smartphone, camera phone, or other mobile device;

- give me a custom URL to display the photos in the album;

- allow me to name and caption all the photos in the album;

- allow me to view the album as a slideshow, download all the photos in the album with a click, or easily share the album on Twitter and Facebook; and

- will even create the code needed to embed the album on a web site.

There are a couple of drawbacks when using the free version of the service. Uploaded photos are automatically deleted after 14 days, so I would advise downloading the photos once they are all gathered or submitted. Also, uploads are limited to 100 MB of photos per month per account or album. For $45/ year, you can remove both these restrictions.

Clint Stephens
Educational Technology Integration Specialist
Southwest Educational Service Center, Utah
Twitter: @sedcclint
Website/blog: http://sedcclint.com/

A Student's View

From Hadley, Grade 9:

This site allows you to add any of your friends to your "lists" so they can see your photos. My friends and I always take pictures on different phones, and it is a pain to send to send via message. This is a much better option.

Why Yogile?

Yogile provides teachers with an easy-to-use online photo album for their students. Because it leverages student mobile devices, it can quickly be incorporated into the classroom without purchasing any new equipment. The fact that Yogile deletes images after 14 days gives teachers and students peace of mind about removing old projects from the web and reduces the overall digital footprint.

Taking It to a Higher Level

- Use Yogile as an assessment tool. Have students take photos to demonstrate their understanding of a curriculum concept. They can upload the photos through e-mail and use the subject line to describe how the image reflects the learned concept.

- Develop your community with photos from a classroom event. Give parents and students the ability to share photos from a party or field trip. All they need is the e-mail address to start sharing memories with everyone in class.

- Create a photomontage in lieu of a report. Students can work in groups and develop a series of photos to illustrate a concept.

YOUTUBE EDITOR

Bird's Eye View: Five Things to Know About YouTube Editor

1. YouTube Editor allows students to "mashup" multiple clips into their own video projects.

2. Video clips can come from student uploads to YouTube or through a library of clips available through the Creative Commons.

3. Videos are edited in a time line format that allows student to trim, enhance, add effects, and more.

4. Students can add titles, music, and transitions to their projects.

5. Completed videos are published to students' YouTube accounts and are shared through the Cloud.

What Is the YouTube Editor?

Source: ©Google 2014

When many teachers think of YouTube, they picture kids watching videos of dogs on skateboards or the always classic "Harlem Shake" remix videos. While it's true there is a lot of interesting content on the video service site, there is also an amazing video editing tool that can transform the site into a video creator.

The YouTube Editor is a hidden gem within your YouTube account that allows users to "mashup" content from multiple sources into a completely new creation. Content can come from the user's original YouTube uploads, or you can sample from a library of videos from the Creative Commons. Projects are assembled in an online editing tool that provides users with the ability to edit clips, add music, or develop transitions and titles.

Once a project is complete, the finished video is published to the user's YouTube account. Students can then submit the final video as a link.

YouTube Editor Features

Source: ©Google 2014

The time line in the YouTube Editor provides you with several different features to edit and create your project.

Video

- Trim video clips by using the sliding crop tool on the video.
- Effects: Choose from a variety of special effects including Auto Fix (basic color and lighting), Slo-Mo, Pan/Zoom, Filters (lots of choices to change to look of your video), and Stabilization.

Text/Transitions

- Many different slide options to create titles including: Centered, Sliding, Zoom, and more.
- Text can be imposed on top of the video as well.
- Many transition options to add in between different clips.

Music/Sound

- Choose from a collection of preset music. (Note: these are real songs, mostly by unknown artists.)
- You currently cannot upload your own music to clips.
- You can trim the music using the crop sliders on the sides of the song.
- Sound from the video clips is still audible with music in the background. You can control volume of the video clips.
- You currently cannot add a narrative track.

Photos

* You can add photos to your project. Upload your own images or use images from the Creative Commons using the search feature.

Adding Video to Your Project

When using the YouTube Editor you'll start by uploading or finding video content from the Creative Commons.

Original Content. To upload your own videos for mashup, it's as simple as going to YouTube and clicking the Upload button. This gives you options to upload previously filmed material or to create a live webcam capture using the camera on your device. Uploading original video content should be complete before starting your mashup in the YouTube editor.

YouTube provides users unlimited upload storage for their videos. The lone caveat is videos can't be longer than 15 minutes or larger than 2 GB if they are in a personal account—this feature can be increased in the account settings. Districts/Schools using Google Apps for Education (GAFE) can upload longer videos as part of their school accounts. The district administrator controls the settings for these accounts.

Creative Commons. The YouTube Editor has a direct search of materials loaded in the Creative Commons. This is a great way to give your students access to materials covering a wide array of subjects and events. Even better, Creative Commons videos allow for students to use the footage without breaking copyright protections. As a teacher, this is great way to instruct your students about the role honoring copyright has while creating digital projects.

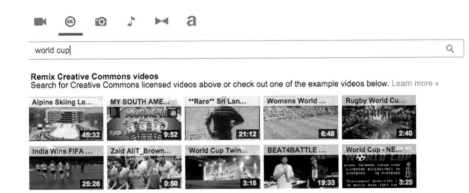

Finding clips in the Creative Commons is as simple as a Search using the provided box. Clips matching your search terms will appear, and you can add them to your mashup project with a simple drag and drop.

Down in the Trenches

Jared Fawson, a geography teacher from Layton, UT, recently discovered the power of the YouTube Editor as part of a capstone current events projects his students completed. Here are his thoughts:

> As a geography teacher, I have been looking for a way to tie everything in that we learn about during the year into one big final project. I have always enjoyed the Zeitgeist videos that Google produces that highlight the most searched stories and events of each year. I decided to incorporate that concept into our class by having students chronicle the major current events worldwide from the start of school to the end, basically August through May. They had to pick events each month that they felt should be included in their final video. They needed to explain why they were choosing to highlight a particular event, what made that event more worthy to be chosen than other events. It can be a real challenge to find the right video editing program to put a project like this together. In the end, my students used the Video Editor to find images and video clips that illustrated their point of view of the past 9 months with regarding major world, national, and local events.
>
> There are many reasons that I think the Video Editor is worthwhile. First, the students get to create a project that they can show the world. Most projects end up being viewed by the student, parents, and teacher, maybe the class, but that is usually it. Using YouTube really does open it up to the world.
>
> Second, students get a project that they can keep. In the past, posters have been an acceptable medium, meaning as soon as project is over it goes in the garbage, plus there is only so much you can do with a poster. Next point is copyright infringement. I think the YouTube Editor does a great job teaching how to be a responsible creator in digital age. Because you are limited to copyright free images, music, and videos, students learn that if they are publishing worldwide they need to make sure they are following the rules.
>
> Finally, and perhaps most important, is the ability to create. I allowed my students a lot of freedom in this arena. They could add

anything to their video that meant something to them, which I felt was important from a creative stance as well as it meant I didn't have to watch the same video 150 times. Each one would be as unique as the students themselves. Students have really enjoyed this aspect of the video editor. They make the final call on edits, clips, and anything they put in or leave out of their video. They also love that others can see their video and they can view what the rest of the class has done. They will do a good job for you; if they know it will be published for the world to see, they will make sure it's worthy of that as well.

Source: Used with permission of Jared Fawson.

Jared Fawson

Secondary Social Studies Teacher

WestPoint Jr. High

Layton, UT

Twitter: @MrJFawson

Website/blog: http://impossible teaching.blogspot.com/

Recommended Tool to Explore: Google Hangouts

This was the best project I have ever had my class do. Everything we did all year tied into it, and there were no questions about why we are learning this or how does this apply. Plus, watching videos instead of reading papers or posters is a great way to end your year.

Heather Chambers is a high school science teacher from Cary, IL. For years she has had her students use video as a tool for creating classroom projects. She shares the impact that the YouTube Editor has made on her students.

When I first started teaching in the fall of 2005, having students create videos seemed like a daunting task, but when given the opportunity (thanks to a great coworker/friend), I jumped right in to give students a chance to demonstrate their learning through technology. In 2005, students all used the same video camera, computers, and program to edit their videos. Now flash forward to 2014, I still have students creating videos to "show off" their knowledge of class topics, but each student has their own device to do so, which can make

(Continued)

(Continued)

Heather Chambers

High School
Social Science Teacher

Cary-Grove High School

Cary, IL

Twitter: @irishteach

Recommended Tool to Explore:
Todaysmeet.com

things a little crazy in the classroom during editing days. I have students edit videos on their phones, personal devices, and school Chromebooks. I needed to find a program that could be used in the Cloud, and that is where YouTube Video Editor comes into play. I learned about YouTube Video Editor at an awesome professional development day and have been using it since.

YouTube Video Editor has been a valuable addition to my "web-tool box" because it allows for video editing in the Cloud for free. A student can edit his or her video on any computer with Internet access, instead of relying on owning expensive software, which really evens the playing field for students regarding access to technology. YouTube Video Editor allows students to add audio, text, transitions, and videos licensed under Creative Commons. It is a great video editing tool for students to easily create, edit, and produce videos.

When I assign video projects for students, I like to push them to demonstrate their learning through creativity. Producing a video not only allows students to be creative, but also pushes their learning beyond their comfort level. I find video projects to be a challenge for students, but in the end they have a product they can share with pride. Offering choices for students connects to their 21st century life because in today's world we have more choices than ever before in history. Today's students need projects and class activities that go beyond a worksheet or poster. They need challenges in the classroom that not only engage them in the content, but also empower them to own their learning. As a teacher, giving students the option to use Cloud-based tools, like YouTube Video Editor, promotes learning and creativity and prepares them for the real world.

A Student's View

Anne P., a ninth-grade student from Utah, commented about her class project using YouTube Editor:

As a student, I felt that using the video editor to make my project was a great experience. It was different from anything I had done before in any of my classes. I learned about important events that happened around the world, in the country and even in our small community. I even learned how to use good and effective sources. But by using the editor to make the video, my partner and I felt like we could personalize it and make it something awesome. We put things in it that we were interested in and that made it extremely fun to do!

Why YouTube Editor?

This a fantastic tool for creating in the Cloud. Students can work on their own footage or use video from a variety of Creative Commons clips. This is a great way for students to explore topics in more detail and they can quickly share their projects with the world by using the published link. The YouTube Editor gives students the tools they want to make fun and creative projects they want to SHARE!

Taking It to a Higher Level

- Create a photo slideshow. You don't have to solely use video as part of your movie project. Using the Photo tool, students can upload images to create an amazing video slideshow. Whether it's a look back at the field trip or an in-depth study of a science project, students can create fantastic multimedia projects!

- Slow it down. Have students film themselves completing a physical task or project. Using the Slo-Mo feature in the editing, you can have students take a closer look at the fine details when reviewing the task. This would work great as part of a PE or FACS class.

- Have students create mashups of two or more videos. This will allow them to do a compare/contrast assignment looking at various elements of the clips including: POV, setting, style, and more.

SCREENR

Bird's Eye View: Five Things to Know About Screenr

1. Screenr works for Mac and PC.

2. No download is required.

3. Screenr plays on iPhones.

4. Users have the option to upload the screencast to YouTube.

5. It's free to use!

What Is Screenr?

Screenr is a web-based service that allows the user to record up to a 5-minute screencast and share immediately on Twitter or save to YouTube. Once users have completed their screencast, they are given a URL that they can post on Twitter, Facebook, Google+, or other services for friends and family to see. The user also has the option to upload the screencast directly to YouTube where they could then share their video and embed it on websites.

Source: ©Screenr 2015

Screenr is Java based, so it will not work on Google Chrome, so make sure you have Firefox or Safari open for this program. Screenr is nice because it does not require users to download any program to record and share their screencast. For educators who are not allowed to download software on their computers at school, this is an important part of Screenr.

Screenr Features

Quick Sign Up

Signing up for Screenr is also very easy if you already have a Twitter, Facebook, Google, or Yahoo account. Just enter in your account information, allow Screenr to access your information, and you are ready to start screencasting. Too often the sign-up process for free web-based tools can be a tedious, but Screenr wants their users to sign up and start recording in a matter of minutes. For the busy educator, every minute counts, and Screenr makes sure not to waste their users' time.

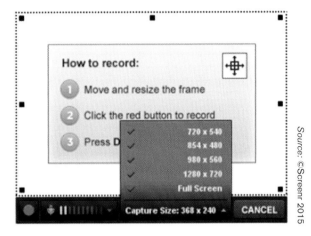

Quick Recording

You just need to hit the record button and you are ready to go. You can size the area that you want to record and just follow the directions.

Once the user starts recording, they have 5 minutes to share their thoughts. The time limit is perfect to allow the user to share the important information without wasting time and dragging on too long. Most students will not watch a video longer than 5 minutes, so this is a great way to get users to focus on the important information or break up longer screencasts into manageable pieces.

Quick Sharing

Once the recording is over, the user will receive the link they can share on social media and they can also upload the video to YouTube so they can embed it into websites and share in other places. Quick and easy sharing is perfect for the busy educator looking to pass on important information to students and staff.

All the videos are saved on Screenr and can be set to private or public. The Public Stream is a great place to look for other screencasts and to take some notes on how to make better screencasts. These videos can stay here or they can be deleted once they are shared to YouTube. If they are deleted, any links to the Screenr video will become broken links, so be careful when deleting from Screenr if you have shared the link publicly.

Down in the Trenches

Kelly Tenkely is the founder of Anastasis Academy and an edtech leader. She uses multiple tech tools in her school to help engage students. Let's hear her story.

When I look for technology tools to implement at Anastasis Academy, I focus on tools that are flexible and can be used by teachers and students alike to make learning more transparent. Screenr fits this bill; it can be used for any subject and age group and is limited only by your creativity in using it! Screenr is a web-based screen recorder that makes it really easy to create and share screencast videos. This is an instant, simple way that students can capture and share whatever learning is on their screen. The resulting video can be embedded on a webpage or blog, shared via e-mail, or downloaded. There is nothing to install or download, you can record from a Mac or PC, the video plays on all devices, and it is free.

As a teacher, it seems like there is just never enough of you to go around. Screenr is a fantastic way to multiply your time and energy. Screencast a lesson so that students can visit the video for some guided learning any time they need it. Screenr can be used with any other technology on your screen. Lead your students through steps in a tech-rich project, record yourself researching a topic, use a drawing application to demonstrate a math problem, or type up instructions and record audio explanations to follow along with. These videos can be embedded in your classroom website or blog, shared through e-mail, or downloaded and saved in a guided-learning folder on classroom computers. In your classroom, use class computers as learning centers that students can visit for support when they get stuck. Students are empowered learners when they don't have to wait for you to get support, and they can move on with their learning! Creating a video bank of screencasts that SHOW students how to learn is valuable. This is on demand mentorship in the art of learning.

Screenr can be used by students as well. Students at Anastasis Academy love sharing their passions with others. Screencasts allow them to be the experts on a topic and guide others through learning. We've had students use Screenr to show others how they learned to code, solve a math problem, beat a game, or create in Minecraft. I love using student videos as teaching tools. Students love being the experts, and peers enjoy watching videos created by their friends. I'm always amazed at the way that learning goes viral in a classroom when students figure something out and share it with others.

Screencasting can be used for more than just tutorials. Students can creatively use the programs on their computer to demonstrate learning through a screencast. We've made videos as a school that show the difference between learning at Anastasis Academy and a more traditional school setting. One of our favorite projects was a screencast of us typing in "school makes me" into Google and recording the auto-fill suggestions. The suggestions are a sobering reminder of the state of education as perceived by students and society. We asked our students to finish the same statement "school makes me." We didn't give our students any prompting or additional information about how we would be using it. Using the same screencast, we embedded the video in a Keynote presentation and typed over the actual suggestions with what students at Anastasis Academy had to say. We used the resulting video to celebrate who we

Source: Used with permission of Kelly Tenkely.

Kelly Tenkely

Founder Anastasis Academy

Centennial, CO

Twitter: @ktenkely

Website:
http://ilearntechnology.com

are as a school (see resulting video here: http://ow.ly/vJYQo). Students have created similar videos to demonstrate learning in a variety of subjects in fun, creative ways.

Asking students to screencast their learning allows you to assess more authentically. When you watch a student solve a math problem, you gain insight into the process. The problem doesn't just get marked as correct or incorrect. You now have the ability to see the breakdown in student understanding and can adjust teaching accordingly. I often ask students to record their process as they research online. Ask students not only to record their screen, but also to talk through their process. I've found it to be useful for me to see how students approach research, but it is also helpful for students to think about their approach.

A Student's View

From Hannah C., Grade 10:

Screenr seems like an extremely efficient way for teachers to show students how to do something on the computer. Being able to see a recording of your teacher's screen makes it so easy because it is just like watching the teacher do it in front of you in class.

Why Use Screenr?

Screenr is a free tool that does not require users to download software to use it. It allows novice technology users to sign up, record, and share their screencasts quickly and easily. Teachers are looking for more ways for students to personalize their learning, and Screenr will allow teachers to share important aspects of their lessons with their students to review on their own time at home to stay on pace with the class.

Taking It to a Higher Level

There are many great reasons to use Screenr as an educator. Here are just a few to consider.

- **Flipping the Classroom.** Flipping the classroom has grown in popularity over the past few years, and Screenr is a great tool to use if the teacher wants students to cover material at home. A teacher can create his or her lessons in 5-minute parts for students to watch at home or on their mobile device. Students can spend as much time as they like on each segment until they understand it fully. Students can control the pace of the lesson and come prepared to class to discuss what was shared on the videos. This saves time for practice and support in the classroom instead of going over the lesson that could leave some students behind.

- **Demonstrating Knowledge.** Students can create their own account or use a class account to demonstrate what they have learned in various lessons. More and more work has become web-based, and students need an option to demonstrate what they have learned using the web tools available to them. Screenr would allow students to demonstrate their knowledge and share it on a public space to receive feedback. Using Screenr would also help students with their presentation skills as they speak and present their information.

- **Technology Support.** Screenr is a perfect tool to show the different steps in using various tools. Too often, time is spent teaching the students how to use various tools, but other stakeholders are often left out of the conversation. Using Screenr to create a step-by-step guide to use certain tools can provide support to parents and guardians who want to help their children at home with their work. Teachers and other staff members could also benefit from watching these videos as well. Using Screenr to create screencasts can save technology support staff hours of time because users can get a head start on understanding tools and how they work before they request one-on-one time.

5

Best of the Rest

Sometimes you just can't fit all the great tools into just four chapters. In this chapter, we explore the best of the rest. Here you'll find tools to help with assessment, presentations, and others—well, we just wanted to include these last few tools because we think they're amazing!

ASSESSMENT

SOCRATIVE

Bird's Eye View: Five Things to Know About Socrative

1. Teachers can create their own online assessments or download ready-made quizzes using Quizlet.com.

2. Assessment can be real-time informal polls, as well as premade summative tests.

3. Students can access assessments online using mobile devices or computers.

4. Teachers create their own classroom where students can access quizzes in a secure environment.

5. Assessment results can be downloaded so teachers can import student scores into their grade book.

What Is Socrative?

Socrative is an assessment tool for teachers and students. It allows teachers to create an online classroom for evaluating students. This is

Source: ©Socrative 2015

can be done with on-the-fly questions or teachers can prepare quizzes using their own questions or import questions from others. Students can access the assessments by entering the teacher's Socrative classroom on any Internet-ready device. Once the instructor starts a quiz or activity for the class, all connected devices immediately start displaying questions and/or responses. When the time limit or quiz is complete, the instructor can access scores and use them for evaluation.

Socrative Features

When you launch Socrative, you'll find that you can engage with your students in a variety of different assessments. In this section, we focus on the different types of quizzes you can create, a competitive interactive assessment called the Space Race, and more.

Types of Quizzes

Traditional formats include T/F, Multiple Choice, Short Answer, and more. Quizzes are easy to create and edit. Quiz questions can be text based or you can also add

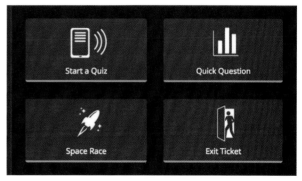

Source: ©Socrative 2015

images to your prompts. You can save quizzes for use in multiple periods. You can also duplicate quizzes if you want to make slight adjustments and retain your original assessment.

Another nice feature is the Import Quizzes option. This allows you to copy a quiz from another Socrative user, or you can import public quizzes from the website Quizlet.com. With over 20,000 quizzes, you should be able to find assessments in a variety of subject areas and grade levels.

Fun Interactives

Space Race is a tool that turns your students against one another in a race against time. Rather than an individual evaluation, Space Race takes your questions and creates a contest where the "best" team conquers.

The teacher has the choice of dividing students into small groups, or you can let Socrative automatically divide the class into even groups. Once the teams are set, the "game" begins with students receiving random questions from a previously uploaded quiz. For each correct answer, the team will see their progress in the form of a rocket ship flying across the screen. Your assessment can run to its completion, or you can set a time limit for the quiz.

Students, regardless of their age, enjoy this type of assessment. Competition generally appeals to many students, and the visual nature of Space Race really motivates students to perform at a high level.

Download the Data

A feature many teachers value is the ability to review student results. You can do this by receiving an e-mail containing a summary of results or instructors can download a spreadsheet containing student scores. The spreadsheet is available as an CSV download, or you can view the data online as part of a Google Sheet.

Once the scores have been downloaded, this data can quickly be imported into most SIS grading programs. This is a huge benefit because it means you don't have to enter scores manually into your district grade book.

Down in the Trenches

Michael Medvinsky, a music teacher, has been using Socrative with his students. Let's hear his take on this amazing tool:

In a classroom where process is valued over product and experiential, collaborative learning encourages learner musicians to look closely, think deeply, and wonder incessantly, the learning may be difficult to capture. I began using Socrative in my classroom to capture snapshots of the learning process and support students' forward thinking. I have found that when learners cocreate short answer questions to use as a reflective tool, their thinking is made visible and any misconceptions arise. The discussions that stem from collaboratively creating questions for Socrative is often rich and relevant.

Source: Used with permission of Michael Medvinsky.

Michael Medvinsky
Educator, Consultant
Bloomfield Hills School, MI
Twitter: @mwmedvinsky
Website: michaelmedvinsky.com
Recommended Tools to Explore: Nearpod, Three Ring, kahoot.it

When learners have created an artifact that shows their understanding of a learning goal, we always meet as a whole class to reflect on the experience before the revision process. I prompt the class with a question such as, "What do you think might be a good question to guide our thinking during the revision process?" This question is a launching point for learners to think about specific questions that are focused on the experiences learning. Times such as these are where learners may also show their understanding through the depth of their questions. I open Socrative to Create a Quiz and choose New Short Answer. I then type the questions suggested from the class. This is the time where learner agency becomes very apparent. The dialogue that is launched from the questions suggested by the class focuses on the process of the learning. As we agree on questions, I add more Short Answer questions and take suggestions from different learners until we think that this quiz is a good representation of our learning. The rest of the class period, or the next time we meet, will be dedicated to each learner reflecting on the previous experience. There is almost always a question about ways to extend their learning or next steps in their project if using Socrative is within the process.

The reports are a valuable tool for educators. I reference the downloaded spreadsheet when meeting with groups of learners when scaffolding their learning, or individual learners when having a conference or meeting with focus groups. These are times in which I listen closely and help question learners toward understanding. This is the time that helps drive my instruction. Socrative has enabled me to understand the process of learning and unique needs of individual learners.

Learn more about Socrative by checking out some reflective quizzes created by some of Michael's fourth- through eighth-grade learners.

SOC-1139775

SOC-740458

SOC-1300650

At the beginning of the school year, Erin Silfer, of Madison, IA, was awarding a set of 30 Chromebooks for her classroom. Erin has been using Socrative's Space Race feature to engage her students and to assess their learning. Here's her take on using Socrative with her students:

Socrative is an online learning tool that teachers can use to create quizzes for students. I use this tool every Thursday. At the beginning of the term, my tenth-grade English II students receive their syllabus. The last couple of pages of the syllabus list the essential knowledge they will learn by the end of the semester. I ask students to look this over on a weekly basis. I test my students on bits of essential knowledge every Thursday using Socrative. I have all my essential

(Continued)

(Continued)

Source: Used with permission of Erin Silfer.

Erin Silfer

Teacher

Madison, IA

Recommended Tools to Explore: Schoology, PowToon, VoiceThread, Diigo

knowledge quizzes on Socrative, and I select the interactive Space Race game.

Students love this Thursday quiz because of the competition aspect of the Space Race game. I break the students up into teams consisting of four to five members. Each member, once logged on to my Socrative class, is assigned a color that indicates which space ship they are in control of. The space ships start moving for every answer they get right. The goal is to be the team that makes it the farthest with their space ship. Even though these are secondary level students, they love this type of quiz! Once the space race is over, I can ask that Socrative e-mail me the results of the quiz. The program will e-mail me an Excel Sheet that contains each group and every question. It will let me know which questions the students missed. I use this as a form of preassessment or assessment of what my students know. If I find that they are missing concepts that we have already gone over, I then know I have some reteaching to do. I can also gain an understanding on how much the students know a concept before we begin that unit, so I don't waste time going over something that they already know well.

It is a fun way to quiz students, and they enjoy the game aspect of it. It is a wonderful way to get data on my students to assess where they are and where we need to go in my classroom.

A Student's View

Carly C., a high school student from Iowa, says,

The space race on Socrative is awesome and fun for students! It encourages competitiveness to learn.

Why Socrative?

Teachers and students love Socrative because of its basic format and ease of use. In a few short minutes, teachers can create robust quizzes or fun interactive tools. Because Socrative can be accessed using any Internet-ready device, it fits in perfectly within a one-to-one classroom. Finally, who doesn't love an easy way to access student data? Socrative results can be exported into formats that are easy to integrate into your school SIS programs. If you're looking for an assessment tool that's fast, fun, fair, and free, Socrative may be the ticket.

Taking It to a Higher Level

● Exit Tickets are a great way to have student reflect on their learning. There are preset activities for you to use, or you can create your own. Exit Tickets help kids share the "Big Idea" from class or provide them a way to set learning goals for the future.

● Using the Quick Question option is a quick way to assess student understanding. You can create a single, on-the-fly question for students. For example, use the True/False option and ask your students the assessment question live (that's right—you have to talk to the students on this one). On the students' device, they will only see an option to mark either True or False. Students will use their device to mark their response to your question. Immediately, you'll see the class results and be able to customize your instruction accordingly.

● For continued learning and ideas check out the Socrative Garden (www.socrative.com/garden). This blog has quick ideas for using the site. There is also a way to share lesson plan ideas with other educators. Finally, you'll find training materials to maximize your use of Socrative.

GOOGLE FORMS

Bird's Eye View: Five Things to Know About Google Forms

1. Google Forms allows teachers to gather data from students/ parents and imports that information directly into a spreadsheet.

2. There are several different question types that can be used as part of Google Forms.

3. Google Forms can be used as an assessment tool using the Add-on Flubaroo.

4. Google Forms offers a variety of templates, and users can build their own templates using images and colors.

5. Data can be summarized quickly in Google Forms using built-in tools.

What Is Google Forms?

Source: ©Google 2014

Originally, Google Forms was a minor Add-on to the spreadsheet tool in Google Docs. It quickly gained popularity as a way for teachers to gather data from students and parents. In just a few minutes, teachers could create a form that allowed them a glimpse into student understanding. Many teachers have also used Google Forms to survey parents and get important information.

Google Forms is easy to use because teachers simply create questions they want others to answer. The questions can come in a variety of styles, each providing different types of data that can be used in the classroom. Forms can be e-mailed to users, or you can provide the URL for the form.

Google Forms Features

- **Questions Types.** When you are looking to conduct a survey or create a quiz, the type of question you ask will have a big impact on the answers you receive. In Google Forms, you can choose from nine different types of questions. These include:

1. Text (for short answers)

2. Paragraph Text (for longer answers)

3. Multiple Choice (one right answer)

4. Checkboxes (can choose multiple answers)

5. Choose from a List (one right answer)

6. Scale (users rank their response numerically)

7. Grid (users can match categories with answers)

8. Date (great for having questions with a date as the answer)

9. Time (useful for question with a time as the answer)

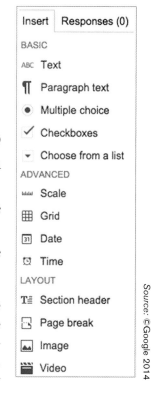

Source: ©Google 2014

- **Layout Tools.** In addition to questions, there are several other features that you can add to a Google Form. This can provide more information or help lay-out your form to help make sense of the content. There are four different layout tools provided. They include:

1. Section Headers (allows you to groups questions together)

2. Page Breaks (helps you organize your form into multiple pages)

3. Images (can be used to help students as a visual aid for a question)

4. Video (embedded from YouTube—can be used as information for questions)

- **Add-ons.** The latest addition to Google Forms is being able to extend your form with third-party Add-ons. These tools give you the ability to integrate Google Sheets as part of your forms and save time and productivity.

   o **Form Notifications.** Make sure you never miss when some-one responds to a form. This tool allows you to enable auto-matic alerts to your Gmail when users submit responses.

   o **Form Values.** Saves your multiple-choice, checkbox, and other questions for future reference. You won't need to con-tinually type in the same questions.

Customize Google Forms

You can now create your own templates in Google Forms. For years one of the biggest complaints about Forms was the limited number of templates you had available. Now, Google has provided users with the ability to customize every aspect of a form. Most important, teachers and schools can upload their own graphic to use in the form's header. This allows schools and districts to use their logos to create a professional and uniform look.

To customize your form, click on the Change Theme button along the top row of tools. You'll see a menu pop up along the right side of the screen, which gives you access to a variety of tools and features. To use a template you've already created, click on the button Choose form near the top of the sidebar menu. Browse to find a form using your custom template and select it. It's that easy!

Quizzes From Forms

A terrific classroom application for Google Form is to make quizzes that can be graded by Google. Once you create a Form with your quiz questions, you'll want to get into the response spreadsheet. Here you'll have the option to install the Flubaroo Add-on. This simple script takes your spreadsheet and allows it to be gradable— as if the answers were run through a Scantron. (How's that for old-school reference?)

You'll need to take your quiz once to create an answer key, and then the rest is run through the Flubaroo wizard in your response spreadsheet. You can choose how many points are available for each question, whether or not to grade a specific question (like an essay question), and you can separate out student information from quiz questions. Once you tell Flubaroo which submission is the answer key, it's off. Within a few seconds, you'll see a new sheet in your spreadsheet; the new sheet is full of graded responses. Just like that you can see which questions work and you'll be able to identify collective or individual understanding.

Down in the Trenches

Diane Cauchy is an educator and curriculum coach from Michigan who has been using Google Forms with her students in several different ways. Following are some examples of how Google Forms has impacted her classroom.

Google Forms is a fantastic paper-less way to collect a variety of information from my students. Because Google Forms can easily be embedded into our class website, I can use them for quizzes or written response items. It's quite effective to assign students an article to read online, and then create a quiz to measure comprehension. Students can even use multiple tabs to switch between the article and the question, which encourages them to go back and reread to answer a specific question. Using the Flubaroo Add-on, Google Forms will even grade multiple-choice quizzes! The paragraph option in Google Forms is also useful for collecting focus questions that require students to analyze and synthesize information from their reading, citing text evidence (ELA-Literacy RI.7.1) for support. Form examples: http://bit.ly/1FZrOGm or http://bit.ly/1JLfn89.

Source: @Lakeshore Photography 2014

Diane Cauchy

ELA Teacher (Grades 7 and 8) and Curriculum Coach

Coleman Community Schools

Coleman, MI

Twitter: @dmcauchy

Website/blog: http://tech4ela.weebly.com/

Similarly, students can also practice identifying supporting evidence in arguments, typing a list of "pro" evidence and "con" evidence (lead in for ELA-Literacy W.7.1). For students who need extra help in formatting essays, Google Forms can provide scaffolding to write each paragraph. After viewing the movie version of a novel, students were asked to write a compare-contrast essay, though some students needed more guidance. Using Google Forms allowed me to provide instructions for each paragraph and a space for students to write (ELA-Literacy W.7.2 and ELA-Literacy RL.8.7). Form: http://bit.ly/1IPrd0P.

Google Forms can also be used in conjunction with other web tools. Using the Fakebook creator from Classtools.net (http://www .classtools.net/FB/home-page), students created a fake Facebook-like page for the main character in a novel. We discussed Hannah in *The Devil's Arithmetic*. Students created a page for her after reading only two chapters. At the end of the book, students could then add and edit the page to account for the character's growth and

(Continued)

(Continued)

change throughout the novel. This required students to think critically and make many inferences. Google Forms became necessary to collect individual student URLs. It was far more accurate to copy and paste the URL into a form rather than writing it down. Using the information, I was also able to create a master list of websites so students could view one another's work (ELA-Literacy RL.8.1 and ELA-Literacy RL.8.3). Student example (beginning of book): http://www.classtools.net/FB/1604-zMpvLa.

A Student's View

David H., a student at the University of Michigan, likes how Google Forms integrates into the other tools in Google Drive:

The flexibility and ease of use makes Google Forms a great tool for surveying and information gathering. Its integration with Google Docs and Sheets adds another really important layer that allows for easy access and organizing of the data. The tool allows for a wide range of survey formats that when combined with the features accessible in the other integrated Google apps makes the information gathering adaptable for just about any purpose.

Why Use Google Forms?

Google Forms has revolutionized data collection in schools. Teachers can survey students and parents with the data all going into a single spreadsheet. It's so much easier to keep track of your information when it's all in one place! Informal assessments are easy to design, implement, and grade using tools like Flubaroo. With the one-to-one classroom ever expanding, Google Forms is a tremendous tool to provide the teacher with quick feedback on classroom activities and content. This is a must use tool for any classroom in the Cloud!

Taking It to a Higher Level

- Use the Summary of Responses under the form menu to get a snapshot of your data. It's a quick way to assess student understanding of a particular topic or a fast view of your parents' collective feelings about an upcoming event. Google Forms takes your spreadsheet data and automatically creates visual charts to represent the data.

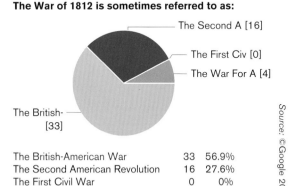

The War of 1812 is sometimes referred to as:

The Second A [16]
The First Civ [0]
The War For A [4]
The British- [33]

The British-American War	33	56.9%
The Second American Revolution	16	27.6%
The First Civil War	0	0%
The War For American Independence	4	6.9%

Source: ©Google 2014

- Have students submit assignment URLs using a Google Form. Rather than having your students e-mail you the link to an online assignment, have the kids copy and paste the URL for their project into a Google Form. This provides you with all the project URLs in one location and really speeds up the grading process.

- Use QR codes to share the link to your Google Forms. With so many students and parents using smart devices, QR codes are a quick way to get the URL for your form out to your audience. Even if you're not in a one-to-one classroom, Google Forms work great because students can share their device with a classmate. Since Google Forms doesn't require a log in, both students can fill out the survey from the same device!

KAHOOT!

Bird's Eye View: Five Things to Know About Kahoot!

1. Kahoot! is an assessment tool that contains quizzes, discussions, and surveys.

2. Users can create their own quizzes or select from a huge library of public Kahoot! quizzes.

3. Kahoot! requires users to have an Internet-ready device to respond to the quiz, as well as a separate device for seeing the questions.

4. Teachers can download quiz results to assess how students performed.

5. Kahoot! quiz scores are ranked by correct answers and fastest times.

What Is Kahoot!?

Source: ©Kahoot! 2015

Kahoot! is an online quizzing tool that engages your students with a competitive twist. As your students answer questions, Kahoot! tracks the students' responses in a real-time leaderboard. Students get points for a right answer, as well as for a fast answer. Students love the game aspect of Kahoot!, and teachers love the ability to assess student understanding.

Kahoot! Features

- Setting up quizzes, surveys, and discussions is pretty straight-forward in Kahoot!, but there are some things that will help you use it effectively.

- Kahoot! questions can have up to 95 characters, and responses can be up to 60 characters long.

- You can embed images or video in your Kahoot! questions.

- Images can be revealed immediately, or you can have your image uncovered in parts as part of the question.

- Teachers can determine the length of time for student responses.
- By default there are four possible answers to your questions, but you can expand to include more choices.

Source: ©Kahoot! 2015

New Type of Assessment

Kahoot! is not a typical quiz tool. Rather than having students all sit quietly answering the questions for an allotted amount of time, Kahoot! will have your students actively engaged in a classroom competition. Each question is loaded up for the class to see and answer at the same time. Students are rewarded with points for correct answers and those who respond fastest get more points.

To get started, teachers create their own quiz or choose a public Kahoot! quiz. After a basic set up, you're ready to share the quiz with your students. Kahoot! displays the questions from your quiz on a shared instructor computer. Students will see quiz questions and the possible responses. Using their own devices, students will click on the correct answer as quickly as possible. Kahoot! provides the class with a leaderboard after each question.

Down in the Trenches

Dan Aldred, a curriculum leader for computer science at the Thirsk School in the United Kingdom, has been using Kahoot! with students for the past year and loves seeing his students engaged. Here is his story:

Question and answer has always had a role in learning, education and quiz shows. All too often your knowledge and often your IQ are measured in relation to your ability to instantly recall the facts and answers on a range of topics. However, these answers can be learnt through practice and repetition. Winning becomes more about memory recall than about understanding.

At school students have always enjoyed a quiz, and this makes them a suitable method of testing understanding and knowledge. In

(Continued)

(Continued)

the past, the traditional paper-based quiz meant that students had to wait until the end of the quiz to see if they had won or to know how well they had performed. If the teacher wished to look at what the students understood or could recall, then they had a mammoth data crunching task ahead of them.

As game shows have introduced audience participation and live interaction, so quizzes have had to adapt to these new approaches. In education, new quiz hardware has been developed, where for around £4000 a school can buy a class set of "a, b, c, d, and selectors" but this is expensive. Schools usually only have one set, which has to be booked out. Feedback and the user experience are still very stationary. Then there was Kahoot!.

Kahoot! works across all platforms, iPads, mobile phones and devices, Android, and variety of web browsers. This means that the majority of schools can set up Kahoot! without any cost. Learners can all access the quiz without the school having to buy any additional hardware. The software is ready to use.

I discovered Kahoot! about a year ago when it was advertised with the strapline 'the most engaging learning tool.' I agree it is. It presents each player with an answer pad and combines multimedia to create an exciting learning environment. Students are extremely vocal when they get a question correct, fist punching the air! When they get the answer incorrect they self-reflect, I knew it was that, this cementing their understanding further. The competitive element is heightened with a leader board, which is displayed at the end of every question. Each student then knows how many points they need and how well they are performing. It is very exciting, and the most basic classroom is transformed into an electric learning environment.

I initially began using Kahoot! as a reward at the end of lessons. I would allow the students to select quizzes form a public menu of over two million. However, I soon realised that my students clearly enjoyed the experience and were learning a lot. I began to create my own quizzes related back to my subject area, developing content to contribute to the shared public bank.

Kahoot! moves students' learning forward in an engaging and inspiring way. Recognising an opportunity, I decided to take this further by asking them to produce the quiz. Each student submits a question and four responses, one of them being the correct answer. This enabled me to test my students' understanding whilst quickly developing a bank of questions for a quiz and allowing students to take ownership and personalise their learning. Interestingly, students also began to stretch and challenge their own understanding by trying to think of and to create the most challenging question, in turn augmenting their learning.

Source: Used with permission of Dan Aldred.

Kahoot! is now fully embedded in my classroom and within the learning environment. We have a Kahoot! most lessons. I use it as a starter to see how much students know about a topic and then run the same quiz at the end of the session to measure how much they now know. Sometimes Kahoot! offers a refresher for say perhaps an intensive theory lesson. Revision for exams is now fun and memorable, and students test their understanding by writing the questions.

Dan Aldred

Curriculum Leader for Computer Science and ICT

Thirsk School

United Kingdom

Twitter: @dan_aldred

Recommended Tool to Explore: http://formtimeideas.com

Finally, Kahoot! provides me with an extremely detailed breakdown of response times to each of the questions. I can quickly scan the colour-coded response and see which questions the class answered incorrectly and therefore which content I need to recap or teach again. I then use this to inform my future planning and support those students whose questions are incorrect or show a misunderstanding of the content.

Kahoot! has been an extremely rewarding tool to use in teaching and learning.

A Student's View

From Paige G., Grade 12:

Kahoot! is one of the best ways to involve students during class. Even in my high school classes everyone seems to really like it. The competition aspect makes everybody want to participate and motivates students to remember what they've learned in class.

Why Use Kahoot!?

Students love Kahoot! The site takes a typical quiz and turns it into a game the whole class will enjoy. Teachers love the variety of tools Kahoot! offers for assessing student learning. With the ability to download student answers, Kahoot! is a great way to determine your class' understanding and teachers can take scores right into their grading programs. Kahoot! is much more than a fun quizzing game.

Taking It to a Higher Level

- Use video as part of your Kahoot! questions. This is a great way to go deeper on a topic. Have your students watch a video from YouTube and use the answer space to provide their responses. Students can share their responses using up to 60 characters.

- Have students create their own questions. This can help reinforce the concepts as students carefully craft questions based on their learning. Once the questions are created, students can share their challenges with one another.

- Find thousands of public Kahoots! in the gallery and share your creations with other educators. This is a great global collaboration, and sharing your quizzes is a great way to enhance learning for teachers and students from across the globe.

PRESENTATION

PREZI

Bird's Eye View: Five Things to Know About Prezi

1. Prezi offers 500 MB of Cloud storage.

2. Existing PowerPoints can be imported directly into Prezi.

3. Prezi works great on mobile devices.

4. YouTube videos can be embedded.

5. There is a free version available for educators and students.

What Is Prezi?

Prezi is a Cloud-based presentation platform that takes the traditional slide mentality of presentations and turns it on its head. Its zooming presentation software allows the user to move in and out of presentations creating an amazing 3D world for the presentation. Since Prezi is Cloud based, presentations can be started and completed on different devices from anywhere in the world. No longer will you need to worry about carrying that flash drive around for your next presentation. Prezi is also great for collaboration. Up to 10 people can work on a Prezi at a time. This is perfect for the classroom looking to explore project-based learning that will have a presentation element as part of the lesson.

Source: ©Prezi 2015

Prezi does employ a freemium model for education. For a fee, users can upgrade to an Edu Pro account or an Edu Teams account. With each level, more options become available to the user. See the pricing guide provided on the next page for more details.

Prezi is a great alternative to using the traditional PowerPoint in the classroom. Students love to use this option because it is Cloud based. Some students do not have PowerPoint at home, so creating a Prezi at school and continuing to work on it at home is very helpful to them. There are many great aspects of Prezi that are worth exploring.

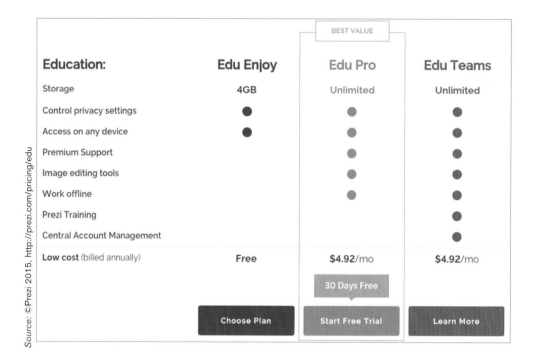

Source: ©Prezi 2015, http://prezi.com/pricing/edu

For teachers, Prezi could be used to flip the classroom. Teachers can embed videos into the Prezi, and the students could move around the presentation, watch the videos, and take notes on what they see. In response, students could create their own Prezi at the end to demonstrate what they had learned. All this can be done from the comfort of a student's home on his or her computer or from any mobile device. Meeting students where they are is an important part of Cloud-based computing, and Prezi is a perfect tool to use to accommodate students on the go.

Prezi Features

- **Collaboration.** Prezi has a collaboration tool that allows multiple people to work on a Prezi at one time. This is a great feature for students who want a dynamic presentation and want to work with a large group. Since Prezi works across multiple devices, collaboration is simple for all users no matter what they are using.

- **Presentation Control.** Prezis can be presented remotely. If a member of the group cannot be there, the presentation can still move forward with control shared with all users no matter where they are. The control of the presentation can be passed to any user, and that is great for groups that are working over great distances.

- **Mobile Apps.** Prezi has apps for iPhone and iPad that allows iOS users to keep creating and sharing their Prezis on the go. For one-to-one classrooms with iOS devices, Prezi is a perfect solution for students who want to create presentations and share from their devices.

- **Templates.** The templates that Prezi offers to its users are great and perfect for any type of presentation needed. Instead of looking at the same few static backgrounds normally found in presentations, Prezi offers many beautiful templates that users can make their own by uploading photos and videos.

Prezi works very hard to keep updates coming and are always looking for ways to make the user experience better and better. Keep on the lookout for updates to Prezi to make your presentation Cloud experience even better.

Down in the Trenches

Starr Sackstein is a high school English teacher, and she works very hard having students integrate technology into their work. She has a great example of using Prezi in the classroom. Let's hear her story:

Prezi for Powerful, Innovative Sharing

Creativity is at the forefront of what teachers do all the time, empowering students to show us what they know in a variety of ways. Presentations are a great way for kids to display their ability to speak and communicate information productively and meaningfully, but they can often be dull and unengaging.

Using PowerPoint or Google Slides, although powerful tools, can be kind of linear and stifling for students looking to really impress an audience. Teaching students to use Prezi offers them the ability to collaborate and create a presentation that visually represents the content they are sharing offering advanced functions that are easy to use and effective.

(Continued)

(Continued)

Starr Sackstein, NBCT

High School English Teacher

NYC Department of Education

Queens, NY

Twitter: @MsSackstein

Website:
www.StarrSackstein.com

One project my students complete in AP Literature and Composition is a Prezi presentation (http://bit.ly/1gKYZQV) on 19th century social issues related to Charles Dickens' England before exploring *Great Expectations*. They work together in pairs to do research and create a small but effective Prezi for a gallery walk of learning. With 2 days to complete the assignment, students address the following standard for research, "Analyze a complex set of ideas or sequence of events and explain how specific individuals, ideas, or events interact and develop over the course of the text." Not only do they seek the historical context, but they also connect it to the literature we are reading to understand the historical impact.

Once the Prezis are ready, the kids set up laptop stations in class. Rotating through each other's work, they take notes and ask questions of the expert of the station. The level of rigor and creativity involved in these assignments far exceed the usual presentations; they speak for themselves. This incorporates and meets the standard of "Integrating multiple sources of information presented in diverse formats and media (e.g., visually, quantitatively, orally) in order to make informed decisions and solve problems, evaluating the credibility and accuracy of each source and noting any discrepancies among the data." Students walk away from this assignment informed and empowered.

With the different navigation and themed looks of presentations, students can select ways to show what they know that is appropriate to content, engaging students in often less than exciting background information. Add to this the fact that the Prezi can be made public to be shared with anyone who wants the information, the students can begin to network their learning.

In addition to exciting classroom work with Prezi, students also present their exit portfolios using this powerful presentation site. Since they don't add too much writing in each of the cells, the students are more inclined to talk to the audience after placing the presentation front and center.

Onlookers can see the amount of work that went into crafting the evidence and enjoy a multimedia approach to discussing a student's learning.

As learning continues to evolve with the technologies available, it is incumbent on educators to model and teach students how to use these useful tools. It is no longer enough to be able to read or write; now, we need to innovate and create to successfully balance the possibilities with content.

Jenny Stambaugh is a fourth-grade teacher and loves using Prezi with her students. She shares a great story of how students used Prezi for project presentations. Let's hear her story:

The way I have used Prezi.com is first by making a presentation myself and incorporating different students reading parts of a selection that honored veterans for an all school meeting on Veteran's Day. This worked because it was easy for the students to be involved, they saw what a great tool Prezi is, and it was very impressive to the rest of the school. Being able to include YouTube as well as pictures and graphics in one easy to use site was exciting. The fact that it is accessible via the Internet is a major draw of Prezi. One no longer has to send a file or have their own laptop to present!

Source: Used with permission of Jenny Stambaugh.

Jenny Stambaugh

Fourth-Grade Teacher

Tuckerton Borough of Education

Ocean County, NJ

Twitter: @jstam4

After our classroom presentation, I did a quick introduction to the Prezi website with the class. I took them on a tour of how to create a simple Prezi and how to add frames and text. From there, I would say exploration on their own was the best way to go. Four students took my challenge and used Prezi.com to present their next project instead of a keynote program. They were more than proud of their work the rest of the class was again motivated to try Prezi the next time.

(Continued)

(Continued)

Another great aspect of Prezi.com is the Explore tab. We have used Prezi many times to find out more about a subject. The topics are varied, anything from Lewis and Clark to dependent clauses! Right now, we are studying the kelp forest and I was able to find a Prezi that was already made, copy it, and then keep the best parts and tweak the rest for our classroom use.

A Student's View

Sam M., college sophomore, described how Prezi keeps him engaged in his college classes:

As a student, I definitely prefer Prezi over PowerPoint. Over the years, PowerPoint has become stale and standard, and to me, it's boring now. Prezi just provides something different that keeps my attention better than PowerPoint. I also like the creative aspects that Prezi provides; to me it seems more suited toward young adults and high school students who are more technologically advanced. Prezi has the "It" factor for students and is definitely more appealing to the creative students who have grown up in the social media age.

Why Prezi?

Whether as a teacher or a student, Prezi offers the user a chance to spice up the traditional presentation. The collaboration element and the 3D environment of the presentation create a great show that will engage an audience who has become accustomed to the slide after slide world of presentations. While there are upgrades available, the free Edu version is perfect for students and teachers looking to make their presentation stand out from the rest.

Taking It to a Higher Level

- The collaborative feature of Prezi can allow students from other classes to create in-depth presentations. These Prezi's can cover a wide variety of topics and can be worked on at different times from their own homes. To really take it to another level, projects with students from other school districts could be created and students could work collaboratively on Prezi's regardless of the time zone or distance. This freedom allows students to create and learn with fewer obstacles.

- Prezi can offer students a great way to share their digital portfolio to the classroom and the community. Prezi allows for users to embed videos and other PowerPoints. Having students create their portfolio presentations with Prezi generates a dynamic way for students to share their work.

- Prezi is perfect for students who love to create mind maps. Prezi will allow users to identify important information and easily move it around to the parts that make most sense to them. With the collaboration aspect, multiple people could work together to flesh out the important aspects of a project by using Prezi as a mind-mapping tool.

GOOGLE SLIDES

Bird's Eye View: Five Things to Know About Google Slides

1. Google Slides allows users to create online versions of their PowerPoint slides or users can create slides from scratch.

2. Multiple students can work collaboratively on a single presentation.

3. Manipulate photos directly in a presentation using a variety of image editing tools.

4. Google Slides has hundreds of new features with over 450 fonts and tons of animations, themes, and transitions.

5. Users can use information seamlessly from Docs and Sheets with Web Clipboard.

What Is Google Slides?

Source: ©Google 2014

Google Slides is a terrific online presentation tool that allows users to create and share their slides in the Cloud. Google Slides can take your existing presentations from programs like PowerPoint and convert them into an editable, online file. As with other Google Drive programs, Google Slides gives teachers the ability to have students work collaboratively in small groups. It is easy for students to share their presentations with others and a great way to have them all working at the same time.

Google Slides Features

• You have over 450 different fonts at your disposal for your presentations. This provides users with a lot of choices to customize presentations.

• There are hundreds of different templates available for user in Google Slides. To find these guides go to drive.google.com/templates. You'll be able to preview the different templates and apply them to your next project.

- Google Slides has seven different animations you can use to add emphasis to your presentation. You can also choose from six different transitions for your slide presentation.

  - Insert a variety of content onto your slides including:

    o YouTube videos

    o Images

    o Drawings

    o Lines

    o Word Art

- Paste content from Docs or Sheets using Web Clipboard. This is a great tool that allows you to create a chart or diagram in one program and paste it into another. The items will remain on the web clipboard for about a month so you have plenty of time to access your content (http://zd.net/1hheYql).

Editing Images in Google Slides

Source: © Google 2014

One of the reasons you want students to create presentations is to help bring content to life with multimedia. While you'll find that Google Slides mostly contains editing tools for your presentation content, you can also find a few creative editing tools as well. Google Slides has a built-in photo editor that provides users with some amazing options. These tools can really add some pizazz to your students' presentations.

Editing your images is simple, just add the image to the slide like normal and click on the picture from the slide. You'll find a crop icon now appears in the toolbar. Not only can you resize the image, but now you also have the ability to crop the image to a shape. Editing the images from the slides ensures that you get the image to your desired size so that your image and content fit together on the slide.

Collaborating and Sharing

One of the best features in Google Slides is the ability to collaborate in small groups. When using software-based tools, you find that working in small groups generally means having one student work while the others watch. Sure, there are ways to work around this using e-mail and other tools, but Google Slides makes collaborating on a project simple. Students just share a project and start working—at the same time!

Have your students create a classroom project with each student adding information on his or her own slide. Using Revision History, teachers can track all the changes made to a particular Google Slide presentation. Use this to help you manage student participation and share feedback with individual students using comments.

Down in the Trenches

Bill Shidler is a fourth- and fifth-grade teacher in Indiana. Google Slides is an incredibly valuable tool for his students to use as the create presentations for class. Let's learn more about the students of Delphi Community Elementary School and Google Slides.

How do we utilize Google Slides in DCES4/5? DCES4/5 stands for our learning community—our Delphi Community Elementary School fourth- and fifth-grade classroom. With all the demands on students, teachers, and parents, I looked toward Google to help streamline what it is we do each and every day. For the last several years, I have begun the year by sketching out my school day. Most people sketch this out via paper and pencil. However, I have begun to digitize what we do. We begin each learning day with a warm-up activity, followed by mathematics, reading, writing, word study, science, and social studies. After this, I create some templates of each day of the week (Monday–Friday). As you know, when you create a Google Slide, you are creating a URL. I take this URL and attach it to my website (http://dces45.weebly.com). From a planning perspective,

I duplicate the week's slides so I have a slide for every day of the school year. I do this for the entire year. As I plan for school, I create each day's slide to relate the day's lesson to the kids (the day's slide is projected on the SMART Board and any changes are automatically updated on the website). What the kids see every day is found on both the SMART Board (projected) and made available to parents with web access as a link on our website (http://bit.ly/1I9YIoY). As each day passes, I push that slide to the end of the running presentation so always that present day is most easily found via the web and as the top slide. Furthermore, students who are absent know exactly where to turn if they miss any schooling. Additionally, all my students have access to laptops so we are moving toward that true one-to-one environment. If this focus page is no longer projected, most of my kids will have a tab open on their laptop so they can see the day at a glance at any time!

Administrators have asked for there to be a purpose to each activity. As I review the state standards (Indiana) and Common Core, I often put a "Students will . . ." statement for each subject area on the presentation. These statements are documented by hand on each child's focus page for his or her benefit. It helps to establish a reason for what it is we are doing during an activity. I also embed and curate content on the presentation so students can click on a link to be taken somewhere via the web for additional information or practice on a skill. All other teachers often mindlessly handwrite their activity's focus on the chalkboard only to erase it at the end of the day and painfully do it time after time—not me, mine are forever found on our Google Presentation. One could see what activities we did every day of the year, and many kids do look back and recall that day based on what they read for that day.

As a teacher, I am able to plan and curate content from anywhere. No longer do I lug home teacher editions (all are found online), nor do I have to write out by hand the activities for the upcoming day, week, or month. Instead of erasing when there is an unexpected cancelation, delay, or more, I can copy and paste from Google Slide into the slide I want. Again, immediately, those changes are seen by anyone reviewing the file online through the website. I have seen many teachers' planners, and I feel sorry for them as they erase, scribble out, and rewrite complex plans—not me!

Another way we use Google Slides is when we had parent-teacher conferences. The students were given what they needed to include,

(Continued)

(Continued)

Source: Used with permission
of Bill Shidler.

Bill Shidler

Grades 4/5 High Ability Educator

Delphi Community Elementary School

Delphi, IN

Twitter: @bshidler

Website/blog: http://dces45.weebly.com

Recommended Tools to Explore:
mybigcampus.com, sentence diagramming

and the students created a presentation that showed their growth during the year. Another example was last year. Every Friday, we had a certain number of kids create a Google Slide about a topic they were interested in. The athletic boys created slides mostly about famous baseball, basketball, soccer, and so on players. The girls about animals or singers. Either way, everyone in our class learned something new about that particular subject.

Still not sold? Our class in Social Studies studied failed colonies, and students used Google Slides to create presentations. Each presentation ranged from 20 to 40 slides. In the end, the colony of Roanoke won. Also, students split into groups and create a presentation about the certain topic they are learning in any of subject in school.

These are all numerous examples of how our class uses (and loves) Google Slides!

Becky Shiring has also been using Google Slides with her students. In her case she uses the tool with adult learners who live in the Washington, DC, metro area.

I teach English as a Second Language at a public charter school for adult immigrants. I have used Google Slides in a variety of ways with my students across many different levels. However, the most powerful lesson I delivered was one in which Google Slides allowed me to differentiate instruction to meet my students at their level.

As an extension to a lesson on the simple past tense, students had to choose a famous person and create a presentation about this person in groups. Within my class, I had varying degrees of English proficiency and computer literacy. To set each student and group up for success, I decided to differentiate each group members' role. I created a skeleton presentation that had a title slide and three blank slides with only the title (early life, why is the person famous, and present day). I assigned each group member a slide by typing his or her name in the notes portion of the slide.

Within each group I had one high level student, one at level student, and one low level student. I assigned the low level student the "early life" slide because this information would be the easiest to find and interpret (date and place of birth, information about education and family, etc.). The high level student was assigned "why is the person famous" because this information would be more difficult to convey. As the students moved through the activity, often the high level students finished ahead of their group members.

Google Slides allowed for these students to navigate to other slides in the presentation and help their fellow group members with editing or content. Additionally, these students could work on the title slide and formatting while other group members finished. The collaboration I witnessed was amazing. The students were so helpful to each other and really took ownership over their presentations. This was evident when it came time to give the presentations in class, and I witnessed students speaking off the cuff about their topic. This is something that is rarely witnessed in an adult ESL classroom where students are very self-conscious about speaking extemporaneously for fear of making mistakes.

I have repeated this activity many times with great success. Most recently, my students created presentations about an African country for Black History Month using the same format. They then shared the presentations to our class Google+ community. I had one group of students who had just finished taking a Microsoft Office Applications class the previous semester, and they insisted on using PowerPoint. I allowed the students to use this tool because it was what they felt comfortable with. However, after they saw how other groups were all working at the same time on one presentation and the ease with

(Continued)

(Continued)

Source: Used with permission of Becky Shiring.

Becky Shiring

Instructional Coach

Carlos Rosario Public
Charter School

Washington, DC

Twitter: @beckyshy

Website/blog:
http://20percentesl.blogspot.com/

Recommended Tool to Explore:
eduCanon

which they were able to share the final product with the community, they had a change of heart. One student told me, "It would have been so much easier to use Google Slides so we could have all worked on it together from wherever we were. One of our group members was absent, and she could have helped us work on it while she was at home!"

Example student presentations:

Vicente Fernandez:
http://goo.gl/rRT8Yr

Martin Luther King, Jr.:
http://goo.gl/h81Xlh

A Student's View

Cynthia, a fifth grader at Delphi Community Elementary School, is a big fan of Google Slides:

I love using Google Slides in our classroom! Especially when I'm absent. If, say I have the flu for two days, I can just go to our class website and click on my teacher's Google Slides and do my expected homework from home. Our Google Slide titled "Focus Page" is a great resource for many of my fellow classmates.

Why Use Google Slides?

Google Slides is a fantastic tool for creating presentations and sharing them in the Cloud. It gives students a platform to work with one another in groups and has the capacity to give students the chance to contribute instead of watch. Google Slides gives you all the editing tools you expect plus has several creativity tools that will surprise you. Overall, this is a great way to put your presentations in the Cloud.

Taking It to a Higher Level

• Embed your Google Slides presentations on your website or blog. This is a great way to share your content with students without having to use e-mail or give students access to another file. Students and parents can find your presentation in its entirety right on your classroom website or blog.

• Use Movenote along with Google Slides. On its own, Google Slides is a great tool for presentations. Mix in Movenote to your Google Slides and you'll take things to another level. Movenote is a plugin for your Google Drive that allows users to create a video narration for your presentations. It's easy to use and helps students give a quality presentation from anywhere. Movenote is a perfect way to get your Flipped Classroom off the ground—just turn on your video camera and you're off and running!

• Using Google Slides on your Mobile device. Recently released for iOS devices, the Google Slides app will bring even more options for creating quality presentations in your classroom.

POTPOURRI

ANIMOTO

Bird's Eye View: Five Things to Know About Animoto

1. Animoto offers free apps for iOS and Android devices.

2. An e-mail address is required to create an account.

3. Created videos can be embedded into other sites.

4. Videos can be shared on Facebook, Twitter, and even uploaded to YouTube.

5. Teachers can apply for a free Pro Account.

What Is Animoto?

Animoto is an online and mobile application that allows users to upload photos and video clips, add words and other music, and create their own video. The free version of Animoto allows users to create up to 30-second videos with access to over 300 songs in the music library to use in the videos created. For an upgrade of $5/month or $30/year, users can create 10-minute videos and can download their work. A Pro account allows users to create 20-minute multisong videos, save videos in HD, access 2,000 commercially licensed songs, and many other business features. For a teacher, the free account would be just fine, but an upgrade to the Plus account could be helpful if they really enjoy making videos for their students.

Animoto allows users to upload photos or videos from their computer or from other Cloud-based applications. This makes creating Animoto videos much easier for people who have photos in many different places. Photos from Flickr, Facebook, Instagram, and other places could be perfect for the video you want to create, and it is nice to not have to search all over the Internet for the right picture. It makes putting together great pictures with nice music quick and easy for the average user.

Animoto Features

Share It Around the World

A nice piece of Animoto that is important to mention is how easy it is to share the work that is created. Once the videos have been assembled by students or teachers, they can easily be shared using various social media outlets. This is perfect for classes that have a joint Twitter account or a class Facebook page so great content can be shared with parents and the rest of the community to see the work that is being created in the classroom. Animoto also allows users to upload their work directly to YouTube and embed the video. By uploading to YouTube or embedding in a class blog, the student work can be seen by thousands of people from all over the world. This is an excellent way to extend learning beyond the classroom and connect students and teachers with a diverse global audience.

Getting Mobile

Another important part of Animoto is the fact they have mobile apps that allow users to create their slideshows on the go. By accessing Animoto on a tablet, students and teachers can create their work from the comfort of their couch after a long day or next to their locker as they wait for their friends after school. It is important for applications to create a mobile environment for users to create because people are on the move. For bring your own device (BYOD) and one-to-one environments, having a mobile app makes Animoto a very attractive tool to use in the classroom. The free version allows users to have complete access to previous work and all the tools they need to create new work.

Since users can now walk around with their device and use Animoto, the possibilities open up about what can be created now that they are unchained from the desk. For teachers, this needs to be taken into consideration when it comes to lesson planning. Students need to be given the chance to move and create as much as possible and the Animoto app does just that. Students should not have to sit in a computer lab and plug away on the traditional slide show when there is a free mobile option that could get them moving around the school. The mobile option for Animoto is a big win for students and teachers.

Down in the Trenches

Karen Chichester is a passionate teacher looking for different ways to have students present their research. Animoto has become a key tool in her classroom. Let's hear her story:

Karen Chichester
English Teacher
Jefferson High School
Livonia, MI
Twitter: @KChichester

Elie Wiesel's memoir *Night* is taught senior year during a larger unit focused on leadership and persuasion. During this unit, we discuss propaganda and how emotion is used to persuade audiences. At the end of the unit, I ask my students to produce a piece of propaganda about either the Holocaust or modern day genocide. I also provide an essay option for the very few who prefer to write. The intent of the project is to get the students to thoughtfully use images and audio to cause the audience to feel something about the topic presented.

After years of watching my students produce slide decks that were filled with words and often read to me, I looked for another option. I found it in Animoto. Once I introduce them to Animoto, the vast majority have chosen to use this site because of its ease of use. I particularly like it because Animoto limits the number of characters that can be used on a "slide" thus putting the emphasis on images and the sound track.

I have tried this both as a team project and as an individual project. The topics (http://bit.ly/1dCfo0t) are assigned by random drawing.

Jefferson High School uses Collins Writing, a Writing Across the Curriculum program. This assignment is graded using Focus Correction Areas (FCAs). These replace a rubric but can be easily be adapted into a grading rubric if you choose. The research aspect is graded separately from the video itself.

Student Examples:

Dachau: http://youtu.be/C4ZOl00yKl0
Buchenwald: http://youtu.be/sipURVcIYDE
Congo: http://youtu.be/QvGEW62ICV4

A Student's View

From Hannah C., Grade 10:

Animoto makes creating presentations way more fun than it has ever been. With all their cool effects and features, I would be excited to do a project.

Why Use Animoto?

Animoto is an excellent tool that allows users to toss out the traditional slide show and create an interesting video that can tell a stronger story. The free account allows students to share what they learned in a compelling visual format that gives them more freedom than the traditional slideshow would allow. Students need to work on their presentation skills, and Animoto is the perfect tool to get students thinking about more complex presentations and get them to move away from the traditional slideshow model that is slowly disappearing in the business world.

The mobile aspect of Animoto is also important to consider. For classes that are BYOD or one-to-one, Animoto is a great free app that students can use on their device and create the work they need for class. It also allows the students to be mobile in the room and school, which can lead to far more interesting pictures and videos using their surroundings as well as the photos they have saved on other connected social media accounts. Teachers can also quickly take photos and create an Animoto for class by simply walking around the room and taking pictures or recording videos. Before the end of the class period, that video could be on YouTube for parents to see. The freedom to move around can lead to some amazing creations.

Taking It to a Higher Level

- Students can use Animoto to create book trailers for their independent reading assignments. This would allow students to share what they loved in the book, but will need to be concise since they only have 30 seconds to share their thoughts.

- With the mobile app, students can be sent on a scavenger hunt and they can place all the pictures of the items they found in an Animoto and then embed them on their blogs or upload them to YouTube.

- Teachers can create 30-second videos to introduce a new book in a mysterious way so students can guess what the book might be about based on the pictures, videos, and music used by the teacher.

PADLET

Bird's Eye View: Five Things to Know About Padlet

1. There is a 160 character limit for Padlet Wall posts.

2. People do not need an account to post on a wall a user has shared.

3. The background can be customized by the user to feature an image of his or her choice.

4. Posts can be placed anywhere on the wall at any size or they can be set to appear in order below the previous post.

5. There is a moderation option that allows the user to approve all posts before they appear on the wall for public viewing.

What Is Padlet?

Padlet, formerly known as Wallwisher, is an online tool that allows users to post content to a virtual wall. Imagine a piece of notebook paper that anyone could see and post whatever content they wanted.

Source: ©Padlet 2015

Users can post notes, videos, pictures, documents, and much much more. This virtual wall can be set to private or shared with the world to become a wonderful collaborative environment. Padlets can also be embedded into websites. They are interactive on the site as well, so that makes it possible for people to just edit the wall from the site, instead of traveling to Padlet to make the changes. Simply put, Padlet is the bulletin board for the modern educator.

Padlet Features

- **Layout.** Padlet allows for three layout types. Freeform allows users to place their posts anywhere on the page. Stream has posts placed below each other on the page. Grid finds all the posts laid out in a grid format on the wall.

- **Wallpaper.** Users can choose from many stock backgrounds or upload their own to the wall. This is a nice feature that allows users to personalize their wall.

- **Privacy.** Users can set the wall to be private with access only granted through e-mail invite. Users can also password protect their wall if that is needed. The wall can also be made public for all to see and use.

- **Unique URL.** When registered, a user can create a wall and choose a specific URL for the wall. This is great for students who might have a hard time remembering URLs for different walls.

- **Mobile.** A great addition to Padlet is the mobile apps. The Padlet app can be found in the Chromestore as well as the iTunes App store. This makes it easy for users to add their notes on the go. Padlet understands that their users are not always going to be behind a desktop to utilize their product, so they made a solid mobile platform so notes, ideas, collaboration, and other Padlet goodness can be shared on a mobile device. For classes that are one-to-one, this makes the use of Padlet that much easier for the teacher and the students.

- **Sharing.** Padlet allows users to share their wall in many different ways. A user can take an embed code and post the Padlet wall on their website. This is great for teachers who want to minimize the number of different sites students travels to on a given assignment. Padlet walls can also be shared using Twitter, Facebook, Google+, and other social media outlets. Padlet also create a QR code for the user if they want to share that with others to gain access to the wall.

Down in the Trenches

Erin Klein shares with us a few creative ways that she is using Padlet as part of her classroom experience. Let's hear her story:

Using Padlet in the Classroom to Collaborate and Create Interactive Sticky Notes!

Lesson Planning

Here is a great example of how I set up a Padlet to organize my lesson plans for the week. These Padlets can be set to private or

(Continued)

(Continued)

public and shared with anyone. These would be easy to share with parents who were curious about what was planned for the week and admins who might need lesson plans for evaluation purposes. The Padlets are clear and perfect for educators looking to visualize their lessons in a digital format.

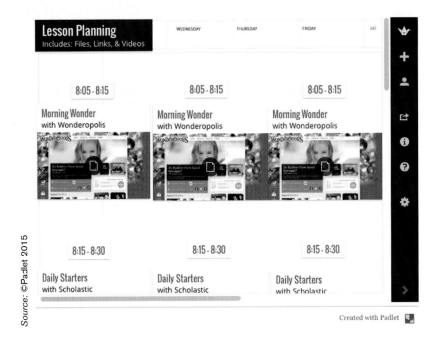

Source: ©Padlet 2015

Geography Map

By placing a world map on the background, students can post notes about where they have been and add media to provide more information about the places they have visited. Students could upload family photos from their own trip or find images or videos on the Internet that represents the part of the world they have visited. This map can be kept active all year, and students can add to it as they travel. It would be fun for class to see the map grow as the progress toward the end of the school year.

Status of the Class

As a reading and writing workshop teacher, I often take "A Status of My Class" before sending them off to work. A quick way to do this

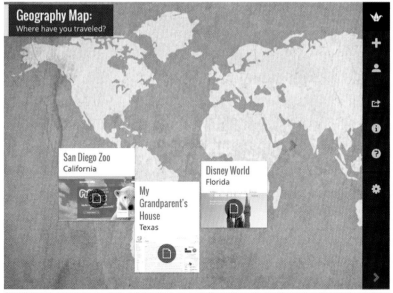

would be to use Padlet. After my mini-lesson, I could put a QR code of the Padlet link up on the SMART Board, have the students scan

(Continued)

(Continued)

Erin Klein

Elementary School Teacher

Bloomfield Township, MI

Twitter: @KleinErin

Website: Kleinspiration.com

it, and be taken directly to the wall. Then, they could post where they were with their process.

As the teacher, after the students have posted to the space, I could drag their comments around to organize them by stages. Stated differently, I can pull all the kids who need a conference together. Those who are revising can be grouped together by simply touching their comment and dragging it closer to the other students who are in revision and so on.

A Student's View

From John B., Grade 11:

Padlet is a great system for classes to use as a whole. It acts as one huge discussion board giving students the availability to stay in touch with their teachers and classmates.

Why Use Padlet?

Padlet is a great tool for classroom use because it is so flexible. It is a blank wall where anyone can place anything they want. That might sound scary, but it means there are limitless options for use. It is becoming harder and harder to maintain some digital spaces that require paid membership or limit the amount of space available per user. Padlet allows users to create as many walls as needed and to store the files they need for as long as they want. Padlet walls can become resources for students for years to come and easily curated by the user to stay current.

Taking It to a Higher Level

 • A Padlet can be created for class discussion, and it can serve as the back channel for the day. These Padlets can then be embedded onto the class website so students can go back to them and study or use as references for essays.

 • Padlets can be created for each student in the class and the links can be shared with all the students. These Padlets can be used to provide feedback for students who present to the class. The posts can be left anonymously so students can leave honest constructive feedback.

 • Padlets are also great for organizing class parties. Students can sign up for the goodies they want to bring and can access the Padlet on their mobile device later in case they forgot what they signed up to bring.

KIDBLOG

Bird's Eye View: Five Things to Know About Kidblog

1. It is COPPA compliant and does not require any personal information from students.

2. Teachers have admin rights over all student blogs and accounts.

3. Parent and guest accounts can be created to allow greater access.

4. Free 100 MB of upload space is available.

5. No ads!

What Is Kidblog?

Source: ©Kidblog 2015

Kidblog is a blogging platform designed to give students access to blogging without having to sign up with their personal information. Based on a WordPress publishing platform, Kidblog allows the teacher to create an online environment where students can practice writing and sharing in a digital format. Kidblog has all the same features of other blogging sites (embedding, commenting, privacy settings, etc.) but is geared toward the K–12 environment.

Kidblog does employ a freemium model that allows educators to pay for more features if they wish to further customize their Kidblog experience. For a price, more student accounts can be created, more upload space can be obtained, and other features that could enhance the blogging experience could be added. Depending on how an educator intends to use Kidblog in their school, the upgrades might be perfect for their situation.

Kidblog Features

• **Safety.** Kidblog offers secure blogging for students of all ages. A teacher can set the security level to allow the entire world to see a post or only the student and teacher to read it.

- **E-mail Free.** Kidblog does not require personal e-mail from students, so elementary students can be signed up by teachers without breaking state and federal law. This allows access to blogging for all ages.

- **Moderation.** Teachers have access to all posts and comments and can choose to moderate as much or as little as they want. The e-mail notification for posts keeps teachers up to date on when a new post is ready for approval.

- **Ad Free.** Parents and teachers do not have to worry about the type of ads their students might see when using Kidblog. No ads will be seen on these blogs, and the entire focus will be on student writing.

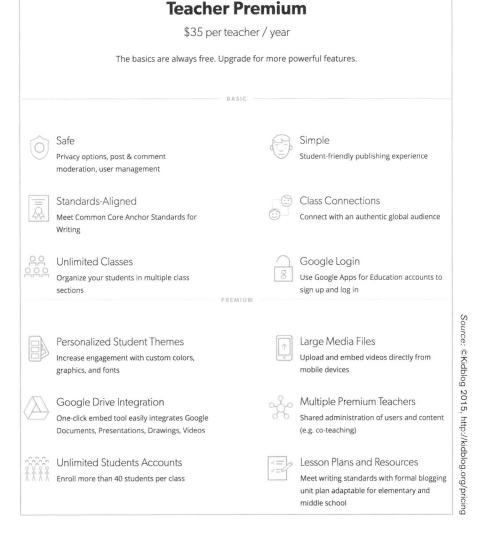

Teacher Premium

$35 per teacher / year

The basics are always free. Upgrade for more powerful features.

BASIC

Safe
Privacy options, post & comment moderation, user management

Simple
Student-friendly publishing experience

Standards-Aligned
Meet Common Core Anchor Standards for Writing

Class Connections
Connect with an authentic global audience

Unlimited Classes
Organize your students in multiple class sections

Google Login
Use Google Apps for Education accounts to sign up and log in

PREMIUM

Personalized Student Themes
Increase engagement with custom colors, graphics, and fonts

Large Media Files
Upload and embed videos directly from mobile devices

Google Drive Integration
One-click embed tool easily integrates Google Documents, Presentations, Drawings, Videos

Multiple Premium Teachers
Shared administration of users and content (e.g. co-teaching)

Unlimited Students Accounts
Enroll more than 40 students per class

Lesson Plans and Resources
Meet writing standards with formal blogging unit plan adaptable for elementary and middle school

Source: ©Kidblog 2015, http://kidblog.org/pricing

- **Tiered Pricing.** More features are available for teachers who are looking to open up Kidblog even more for their students. More teacher accounts, larger file size, more storage space, unlimited students accounts, and much much more.

Down in the Trenches

Maria Selke is an Elementary Gifted Resource Teacher from Pennsylvania and a pop culture junkie looking for different ways for kids to express themselves. She has many great stories to share of how her students have written amazing things and created great projects. Let's hear her story:

I spend a good deal of time over the summer thinking about my students. What can I add in this year to better meet their needs? Whether I am traveling, reading, watching movies, or even just hanging around the house, the back of my mind is always whispering, "How could you use this?" Blogging has become a huge part of my writing life, so naturally I wondered if I could incorporate the thrill of having an audience into my classroom. Wouldn't their own writing lives become more exciting—more joyful—if they were writing for more than just their teacher?

What I Need

As an elementary teacher, I need an environment that allows me to shelter and guide my students in this first digital community. I need to be sure I can limit who can post and comment so that parents will know their child is safe. I also wanted a site that would give students some creative freedom to manage their content and easy access to their classmates' posts so that they have an expanded audience for their writing. As an added bonus, publishing and commenting on our class blog builds many of the skills required by the Common Core Standards.

What Kidblog Provides

Kidblog has the perfect mixture of increased audience size and teacher control. I felt comfortable asking my parents to give permission for their students to blog this year, because I could promise that I had the reins. Kidblog allows teachers to determine who can write, read, and comment on posts. I used fairly restrictive settings. My class was connected to two other classrooms and could only read and respond to one another's posts. Posts and comments would only go live with my approval. There were several times that these settings allowed me to have a quiet talk with students about their digital citizenship skills before posting their writing for the class to see. Making mistakes is part of the process, and this way I can guide and support them in their first steps.

Kidblog also gives students a selection of templates to try out for their individual blogs, if you have the paid subscription. My students loved this chance to express their style, and it gave us a way to explore some elements of graphic design. They played with fonts and colors in their posts. Sometimes it meant that a post was hard to read, but that was an excellent lesson.

What We Write About

Our blog is always available for students to write free choice posts. This year, some of them have recruited friends into comics groups, written poems, and shared favorite books. When we had a "Battle of the Books" in March, our Kidblog page hosted the links to each match and many persuasive blog posts on the merits of favorite titles.

My reading groups, though, have weekly assignments. As we read novels, they choose which response prompt they post to the blog. After I taught guidelines for creating conversations through comments, their weekly responsibilities also included commenting on someone's post. Since I'm also responsible to have my students learn higher level vocabulary and idioms, I decided to increase the fun factor. Each week, I offer a word and a phrase, along with several creative response types. I expect my students to learn the meaning and then use it in poetry or prose. Many parents and students told me how much they enjoyed the creative freedom these assignments allowed.

What the Kids Say

When I asked my fifth graders for feedback on using Kidblog this year, they all shared that they enjoyed being able to complete their assignments on the computer. It seems that losing papers (and getting them wet!) is a concern for many, and having access to their tasks even if they left a notebook at school was a huge help. Several mentioned blogging being a much more motivating way to practice typing skills,

(Continued)

(Continued)

Maria Selke

Elementary Gifted
Resource Teacher

West Chester, PA

Twitter: @mselke01

Website:
http://www.mariaselke.com

which will be vital for them in middle school. Some shared that they wanted more font selections and that tagging posts and navigating their dashboard was sometimes confusing. I'll need to dedicate time this summer to finding or creating tutorials in those areas.

If you are looking for a way to incorporate blogging into your classroom, Kidblog is a fabulous tool. With the flexible level of control and the ability to determine how large your community will be, Kidblog will work for almost any age group.

Mary Beth Hertz is an Art and Technology Teacher and Technology Coordinator at the Science Leadership Academy at Beeber in Philadelphia. She has approached technology integration in many different innovative approaches. Let's hear her story:

One of the essential aspects of learning in the classroom is writing skills. Many teachers have students keep journals or write stories and in some classrooms, students even publish their own work. Now, what if all the writing that students did could be easily edited, published, and shared not only with their classmates, but also with other classes and even the whole world? That is the power of blogging.

One of the easiest blogging platforms for teachers is Kidblog, a free blogging platform that allows teachers to create class blogs for their students. Kidblog allows teachers to create a class blog on which each child has their own blogging space. Teachers can create these student blogging accounts without needing an e-mail and the teacher can set the username to something discreet that will not give away the name of the students, especially if they are very young. In addition, when students access the blog to log in, they choose their name off of a list rather than having to type in a username each time. For anyone who has worked with young students, this is a godsend.

I have used Kidblog most extensively with third graders here in Philadelphia. The students I worked with learned a lot more than just writing skills. They learned and honed a lot of 21st century skills such as typing proficiently, formatting text, proper punctuation and spacing between words and punctuation, uploading files, and perhaps most important, they learned how to interact respectfully and effectively with each other online.

One of the most exciting projects we completed was a research project on an animal. Students learned how to use keywords to do Internet searches, and they learned how to pull information from online sources. They turned their notes into a paragraph, and they shared what they had learned about their animal through their blog. Students were then able to read each other's research and leave comments and ask questions of each other. Since I taught two separate third-grade classes, the two classes even got to read each other's blogs and leave comments and ask questions.

This project tied directly into the Common Core Standard, Research to Build and Present Knowledge, as well as many of the Language Standards tied to demonstrating command of language conventions such as spelling, punctuation and capitalization, especially since they were reading and writing nonfiction texts.

Blogging with students does, of course, come with its challenges. The research project took over a month from start to finish, though we only worked on it 2 to 3 days a week. Students also varied widely in their literacy skills, so for some students, researching and writing was simple, but for others, I had to modify the assignment to make it more within their reach. In addition, doing our work digitally required that students practice typing faster and learn how create certain punctuation marks. It was also vital that we spend time discussing digital citizenship and practice respectful

Source: Used with permission of Mary Beth Hertz.

Mary Beth Hertz

Art and Technology Teacher and Technology Coordinator

Philadelphia, PA

Twitter: @mbteach

Website: http://mbteach.com

commenting before we began. We actually "blogged" and "commented" on paper before we ever typed a single word on the computer.

(Continued)

(Continued)

The biggest hurdle that a teacher will face is, however, access. If the teacher does not have access to a class set of devices, blogging becomes more difficult, but not impossible. A teacher could designate a blogger of the week so only one student is blogging at a time, or have students work at lunch to type up their blogs. They could work in conjunction with the media specialist or computer lab teacher to have the students complete their blog posts during those classes.

Overall, blogging with students is a powerful experience and Kidblog's simple platform, easy setup, and intuitive interface makes accessing this powerful tool easy for students of all ages. To see some of our blog posts about our animals, you can go to http://kidblog.org/AFPCSTaroff/.

A Student's View

From Grace S., Grade 10:

I feel like I'm part of something when I blog. I get to put my ideas out into the world and share my experience.

From Halle M., Grade 10:

Blogging is the best and easiest way to spread out progress with our 20 Time Projects. It helps me reflect on my project, while also being able to share it with the world.

Why Use Kidblog?

Kidblog is an excellent tool for educators looking to introduce students to the world of blogging. Educators can control the blogging environment as much, or as little, as they want as they guide students through the new world of digital media. Uploading Google Apps, embedding videos, commenting on posts, and many other digital skills are crucial for students to learn to be successful. Kidblog is an excellent platform to start teaching students these valuable skills. It offers students the chance to explore writing in new and exciting ways. If you are looking for a way to introduce blogging to your students, Kidblog might be the tool for you.

Taking It to a Higher Level

- Students can use Kidblog as a way to document their projects. While students work on various projects, they can share their progress with the rest of class and the community by leaving updates on their blogs. The commenting features allow others to provide feedback to these students and encouragement as they work to complete their project. Students can upload photos and videos to fully document their work and interact with others reading their blog. This is a great way to keep students engaged in longer projects.

- Blogging stations can be set up in the classroom, and Kidblog could be used by students to take class notes. Students would sit and document the class discussion on individual blog posts that could be reviewed by students who were not in class or wanted to compare their notes against other students. This is great at keeping students engaged in the class discussion and allows students to review notes and share their thoughts with others in the class.

- Student reflection is very important and Kidblog is a great tool for students. Too often, students complete work and just move on to the next piece of work. By giving students a place to reflect on Kidblog, they will have an opportunity to really think about learning and how they did on individual assignments. Since Kidblog allows the teachers to adjust the privacy settings, these blog posts could be set to be viewed by the student and teacher only. Encouraging students to reflect is key if educators want to students truly grow and advance in their learning.

Conclusion

Next Steps

As you come to the end of this book you may be asking yourself, What next? How can I take all these tremendous resources and begin using them in my classroom or school. This last chapter takes a closer look at how two different groups, teachers and administrators, can move forward building their classroom in the Cloud.

For Teachers

After so much great information, it's easy to look around and wonder where to start. The most important thing to remember is that you cannot do everything at once and be an expert. There are certain steps you can take to ensure that you utilize Cloud-based technology to the fullest extent to benefit you and your students.

Explore Tools

This book gave you many great examples of the different Cloud-based tools that are out there to use for yourself or with students. It is now time to explore these tools in depth. It can be scary to explore a tool on your own, but it does not have to be. There are many great tutorials on YouTube that are worth checking out to give you tips on getting the most out of the tool of your choice. Spend time getting used to the basic functions so that you can share with students and help them with their questions. Do not feel like you have to become an expert on the tool and present on it at conferences. Take your time and get the most out of the tool. Once you feel like you have a good understanding of a tool, think about all the different ways it could be used in your classroom.

Never try to build a lesson around a specific tool. The content needs to remain front and center, and the tool is just an additional way to share the content or allow students to consume the content. Just using the tool to use the tool will not make a significant difference in student engagement or learning. Beginners to technology integration sometimes spend so much time focusing on the tool that they forget to make sure that the curriculum is fully covered in class. The bells and whistles can be nice, but the students still need to understand the material at the end of the day. The implementation of these new Cloud-based tools should be seamless for the students, and the best way to do that is to make sure the content is first and the tool fits nicely with what you want to accomplish for the lesson.

Reach Out

It is important to understand that you will not have all the answers and that the best answers might not be on YouTube or Google. It is key for you to reach out to experts and meet them where they are. Twitter is an excellent place to meet teachers who would be more than happy to share how they have used various tools in the classroom. Teachers who are on Twitter are there because they see value in connecting and sharing. Sending tweets for help will always get a reply from multiple teachers looking to support you as you look to enhance your lessons with technology. Twitter is not the only place you can find great teachers though. Blogs and other websites are filled with great resources that are worth checking out. Many great teachers share their work on their sites so others can see examples of great lessons as well as the lessons that did not work. It is important to read these good stories, as well as the bad ones, because it can help you avoid making the same mistakes others have made.

You are not alone in your quest to integrate technology into your classroom. If you are hesitant to reach out on Twitter or comment on blogs, look around your building. There are many teachers trying to do the same thing, and it would be great to work together as a team to try new things and support one another as you look to shake things up in your classroom. Get coffee in the mornings and share the cool new tools you are exploring and trade stories on how you intend to implement them in the classroom. These meetings can really help promote the use of technology in the classroom and will help students as they see more of their teachers using the tools in the classroom.

Survey Students

Take a moment and talk to your students to see what type of access they have at home. Part of using Cloud-based tools is the ability to use them at home and at school without the fear of losing work. If many of your students do not have access to a computer at home, it could make using any form of Cloud-based technology very difficult for students. Do not forget to ask students what type of access they have on their phone. Many students have great phones that can access the web and even download the app versions of many Cloud-based tools out there. While students might not have a desktop computer or a laptop, they might have a phone that allows them access to the tools that you want to use. Make sure to take time and see that the tool you want to use has a mobile version so students can access the application on the go to make working easier for them.

Check Availability

An important step to take when implementing a new tool in your classroom is to make sure that it is available in your building or district. Sometimes something might be available for teachers but not for students. Make sure a student is able to access the sites from their user account as well. This access is key if you want to make the most out of Cloud-based tools. There might be tools that are blocked in your building or district, but do not let that stop you. It is easier to block things than let them sit open for students or teachers to access. If the site you want to use is blocked for students or teachers, get ready to fight the good fight.

"Why" is most often heard when a teacher wants to access a site that has been blocked by a district. Admins or tech directors will share all the fears they have about letting students have access, and it is important for you to have all your positive reasons ready to show them the power of Cloud-based technologies when used in the classroom by students and teaches. Look for policy that forbids the use of these tools. If the policy does not exist, point that out to them. Be warned, that might mean you will be drafted onto a committee to write new policy concerning Cloud-based technology. At least then you can get to use all the tools since you wrote the policy. The only way new technologies are going to be made available to students is when teachers push for their inclusion in the classroom.

Expect Failure

Expect for the first time you use the tool in front of your students to be a bit of a disaster. As many veteran teachers know, the first time a lesson is given to students, it does not go exactly as planned. The unexpected always happens, and you are left wondering what to do next. It is okay to fail in front of your students as long as you do not give up. Technology can be fickle at times, and it is important for students to know that. Take any problems in stride and use them as teachable moments. Take notes of the errors that tool placed and remember how to address them for the next class. The more you use the tool, the better you will get at problem solving the next time something completely different happens. Something not working correctly should be an expectation when it comes to technology. Most tools will not cause problems, but even the best sites will have a hiccup from time to time. Be prepared to troubleshoot the issue and move on. Just like you want your students to deal with adversity and come out on top, expect the same for yourself when it comes to tech integration.

Share Out

Once you have had success in using your Cloud-based tool in your classroom, do not be afraid to share the amazing things you are doing with others. These can be people in your building, followers on Twitter, or readers of your new blog. If you see the value in using that particular tool in your class, advocate for others to do the same. The more people who use these tools in the classroom, the better prepared students will be for the world around them. You do not have to be an expert to share how a lesson worked. Cloud-based tools allow everyone to have a voice, so it is important for you to use it when you have something exciting to share when a lesson worked. Your shared lesson could be the one that inspires another teacher to give Cloud-based technology a shot in their classroom.

For Administrators

Administrators play a vital role in the successful implementation of technology tools within schools and districts. It's one thing for a principal or superintendent to unlock a website or provide funding for new technology tools, but it's a game changer for the culture of learning when administrators are the ones leading the charge. Here are some basic ideas for helping administrators adopt Cloud tools in their schools.

Professional Development

Once you've uncovered all these great Cloud tools for learning, there is a strong tendency to want to mandate your teachers begin immediate implementation. Of course, you've seen the power of having students creating and collaborating online so you want to have this happen now. Before you can change the ways in which your schools educate students, you need to have the buy in of your teachers and faculties. One of the best ways to achieve this is through training.

Think about it—no one wants to be forced to use a tool or site that they don't understand. Teachers want to incorporate innovative ideas, but they want to have a sound foundation in the tools and resources before they jump into the deep end of the edtech pool. Providing ongoing professional development is a great way to support your teachers in every stage of technology integration.

Patrick Greene, a professor of education at Florida Gulf Coast University in Fort Myers, FL, provides the following idea for implementing new technologies into the classroom. "There's a two-step process to integrating technology into the curriculum," Greene explains. "First, teachers must learn the hardware and software; then they must learn to integrate it. The culminating activity should be the development of a comprehensive plan that each teacher writes for implementing technology-enhanced lessons in the classroom" (Star, 2009). As you plan your professional development trainings with your faculty, be sure to work with teachers and ask for their input. Use teacher feedback to assess what their instructional goals are and then help them learn about Cloud tools that can provide educational support in meeting their learning objectives.

Network With Other Administrators

Just as your teachers are learning from and collaborating with one another, it is important for administrators to reach out to one another and share your stories. Administrators from across the world are struggling with the same issues you are when it comes to technology integration. Whether it's funding, privacy, motivation, and so on, there's another principal who's been down the road before. Look for ways to connect with others and be willing to share your experiences.

Eric Sheninger discussed the importance of administrators connecting with one another,

> As connected educators, we're able to take advantage of
> a dynamic resource to connect with a vast network of

educators. We can get some of the best ideas and pick the best brains of people doing the same job we are, serving the same students, in the same types of communities. (Connected Educators, n.d.)

Model the Tools in Your Practice

There is no learning tool more powerful in education than that of example. When a principal schedules a training for the teachers and immediately leaves the room once the workshop begins—a message is sent. Conversely, teachers and faculty will see the power of a connected administrator when that principal or superintendent leads the way in technology integration.

Cathy Camberlain, a technology consultant in the Oswego City School District, describes the important role a principal plays in setting the climate for powerful PD,

> Principals play a big role in setting the climate of a building. Teachers who are on the fence—or think they don't have time to get involved with technology—think twice when they sense a positive attitude on the part of the administration. (Star, 2009)

This doesn't mean that administrators have to use Twitter, Facebook, Vine, and Pinterest all at the same time. It's not important which tools a connected principal chooses to use. Rather, it's about creating a climate in which technology is part of practice. Look for ways to model the tools you want your teachers and students using. Try setting up a collaborative Google Doc for the next faculty meeting instead of sending out an e-mailed agenda. Send out a tweet about an upcoming school event. Create a Yogile photo album with pictures from a recent school activity. Teachers and students will notice the ways in which administrators practice what they preach, and they will be more willing to follow a good example.

Set High Expectations

As we've seen, administrators have a huge influence in the overall success and academic climate within their schools. It is important to expect your students and teachers to reach for high levels when it comes to learning objectives. Using technology in the classroom isn't something you can do every once in a while. Rather, there needs to be a formal strategy in place based on schoolwide expectations.

Be consistent and maintain the same standards for all your teachers. You shouldn't use the excuse that "so and so doesn't need to use Edmodo because they aren't good at technology." Sure you need to be sensitive to the needs of your staff, but if you believe a tool or program will improve the overall learning of your students, then you need to ensure all teachers are striving to succeed.

Be Willing to Try

Every tool isn't going to work the way you planned. Not all teachers will be on board with the transition from Microsoft Office to Google Drive. That shouldn't deter you from implementing new tools and ideas. Sure, you need to be prepared and have a plan for a more successful rollout of technology. The bottom line is still a willingness to try and the fortitude to learn from your mistakes. You are the one who will need to stand up for the pedagogical reasons for unlocking a website or purchasing a tool. You are the one who needs to balance the importance of data security with the value of collaborating with a global community. You can be an agent for change, but only if you're willing to try.

Closing Thought

An important thing to remember is that tools will come and go, but the application of the concepts will remain the same. As you explore exciting new tools, always make sure the focus is on improving the education for the students. If that is always the first aspect of technology integration, it does not matter what tool you choose to use.

The focus of this book has been to show you ways to incorporate learning skills and modern tools to build a classroom that can take place anywhere. Learning shouldn't be something that only takes place between Monday and Friday, from 7 a.m. to 3 p.m. It doesn't have a specific address, and it isn't confined by limits of gender, race, or background. The classroom in the Cloud truly embodies the best aspects of learning and technology; that is, students can learn anywhere, at any time, from anyone, and with whatever tools they have. Having read this book, you are now poised to guide the students on this adventure through the Cloud.

Resource

If You Like That, Try This

Over the course of this book, we've explored a variety of Cloud tools to help you and your students get the most from learning and creating in the online world. We know that not all the tools we've suggested will work for you in your individual situations. Maybe a district filter will prevent access to a particular site. Perhaps there is a cost issue that has made some tools beyond reach. Even the age of your students may keep you from trying one tool or another.

Below you'll find alternatives to our suggested tools. This is not meant to be an exhaustive list, nor do we intend to give you detailed explanations for each alternate tool. Rather, this list is meant to give you choice—another option should you encounter a roadblock in taking your class to the Cloud.

	Suggested Tools	Alternative Options
Storing in the Cloud	Dropbox Google Drive Evernote	OneNote Google Keep Box.net Pocket
Communicating in the Cloud	Twitter Remind Google Hangouts	Shindig ooVoo Skype

(Continued)

(Continued)

	Suggested Tools	**Alternative Options**
Collaborating in the Cloud	Google Docs Edmodo Wikispaces	pbworks Wix Weebly Wikia Wikidot Ning Canvas for Teachers
Creating in the Cloud	Instagram Yogile YouTube Editor Screenr	Imgur Vine Pixlr WeVideo Flickr MoveNote
Best of the Rest in the Cloud	**Assessment**	
	Socrative Google Forms Kahoot!	PearDeck Poll Everywhere Geddit
	Presentation	
	Prezi Google Slides	Canva SlideShare LucidPress NearPod
	Potpourri	
	Animoto Padlet Kidblog	Adobe Creative Cloud (Fee based) Blogger Adobe Voice Educreations

References

Asher-Schapiro, A. (2013, June). *Cloud technology forecast: Sunshine with chance of showers*. Retrieved from http://districtadministration.com/article/cloud-technology-forecast-sunshine-chance-showers

Brownstone, S. (2013, April 30). *Parents grill Department of Education over private student data cloud*. Retrieved from http://blogs.villagevoice.com/runninscared/2013/04/inbloom_data_student.php

Catalano, F. (2012, July 3). *How will student data be used?* Retrieved from http://blogs.kqed.org/mindshift/2012/07/how-will-student-data-be-used/

CloudTweaks. (2012, September 13). *Effective ways cloud computing can contribute to education success.* Retrieved from http://cloudtweaks.com/2012/09/effective-ways-cloud-computing-can-contribute-to-education-success/

Connected Educators. (n.d.). *Interview with Eric Sheninger, principal.* Retrieved from http://connectededucators.org/profiles/interview-with-eric-sheninger-principal/

Educational Technology and Mobile Learning. (n.d.). *Digital differentiation tools for teachers.* Retrieved from http://www.educatorstechnology.com/2013/04/digital-differentiation-tools-for.html

Edutopia. (n.d.). *NIST publishes final version of cloud computing definition.* Retrieved from http://www.edutopia.org/groups/science-technology-engineering-mathematics-education/80873

Fink, E., & Segal, L. (2013, June 28). *Your child's data is stored in the cloud.* Retrieved from http://money.cnn.com/2013/06/28/technology/innovation/inbloom/index.html?hpt=hp_t3

Frontline. (2010, February 2). *The new digital divide.* Arlington, VA: Public Broadcasting Service. Retrieved from http://www.pbs.org/wgbh/pages/frontline/digitalnation/learning/schools/the-new-digital-divide.html?play

Hausman, A. (2013, June 19). *Implications of the cloud in the classroom.* Retrieved from http://www.cloudtweaks.com/2013/06/implications-of-the-cloud-in-the-classroom/

Jackson, S. (2013, December 16). How technology can encourage student collaboration. [Web log post]. Retrieved from https://www.commonsensemedia.org/educators/blog/how-technology-can-encourage-student-collaboration

Mitra, S. (2013, April 29). *We need schools . . . not factories.* Retrieved from http://www.huffingtonpost.com/sugata-mitra/2013-ted-prize_b_2767598.html

Segal, L., & Fink, E. (2013, March 8). *Bill Gates' classroom of the future.* Retrieved from http://money.cnn.com/2013/03/08/technology/innovation/bill-gates-education/index.html?iid=EL

Starr, L. (2009, September 23). *The administrator's role in technology integration.* Retrieved from http://www.educationworld.com/a_tech/tech087.shtml#sthash.zixBWV0c.dpuf

The White House. (n.d.). *ConnectED: President Obama's plan for connecting all schools to the digital age.* Retrieved from https://www.whitehouse.gov/sites/default/files/docs/connected_fact_sheet.pdf

Index

A SAGE Company

CORWIN HAS ONE MISSION: to enhance education through intentional professional learning.

We build long-term relationships with our authors, educators, clients, and associations who partner with us to develop and continuously improve the best evidence-based practices that establish and support lifelong learning.

Solutions you want. Experts you trust. Results you need.